What Makes Switzerland Unique?

Also by Richard Wildblood:
What Makes Switzerland Tick?
The Book Guild Ltd (1988)

WHAT MAKES SWITZERLAND UNIQUE?

Richard Wildblood

Foreword by
Mr J. R. Rich, C.M.G.
British Ambassador to Switzerland 1985-1988

The Book Guild Ltd.
Sussex, England

The Book Guild Ltd.
25 High Street,
Lewes, Sussex.

First published 1990
Richard Wildblood 1990
Set in Baskerville
Typesetting by Cable Graphics
Eastbourne, Sussex
Printed in Great Britain by
Antony Rowe Ltd.,
Chippenham, Wiltshire.

British Library Cataloguing in Publication Data
Wildblood, Richard
What makes Switzerland unique ?
1. Switzerland, history
I. Title
949.4
ISBN 0 86332 505 X

CONTENTS

FOREWORD

by
THE BRITISH AMBASSADOR TO SWITZERLAND 1985-1988
MR J R RICH, C.M.G.

Richard Wildblood has done it again! In *What Makes Switzerland Unique?* he has written an admirable sequel to his earlier book *What Makes Switzerland Tick?*.

It is all about unity in diversity. The author sets out in plain language the complex mechanisms of commune, canton and confederation and the sometimes troubled history that lies behind them. The book is an open invitation to the reader to look deeper into the detail of the rich cultural and historical kaleidoscope of Swiss life.

The Swiss usually maintain that the confederal solutions which they have found to their problems are not for export but are the home-grown product of their own particular circumstances. While that may be true as a whole, many of the more successful features of the Swiss experience offer interesting lessons to others.

The Federal Letter signed by the men of the three Forest Cantons in August 1291 was one of the milestones in the evolution of western democracy. In 1991 the Swiss Confederation will celebrate its 700th anniversary. The appearance of Richard Wildblood's book is well timed.

John Rich

7

ACKNOWLEDGEMENT

The writer wishes to express his indebtedness to the following Swiss Federal Government departments for the information they have given him:

Die Eidgenössische Finanzverwaltung
   (Federal Finance Administration)
Die Eidgenössische Steuerverwaltung
   (Federal Tax Administration)
Das Bundesamt für Gesundheitswesen
   (Federal Health Department)
Das Bundesamt für Sozialversicherung
   (Federal Office of Social Security)
Das Bundesamt für Bildung und Wissenschaft
   (Federal Office of Education and Science)

He is extremely grateful to the following members of the Lenk community for their co-operation and help:

Herr Hans Rudolf Freidig (President of the Commune)
Herr Walter Tritten   (Vice-President of the
                            Commune Council)
Herr Ernst Rieder   (Clerk to the Commune)
Pfarrer Paul Aebisher
Herr Emil Buchs
Frau Rösli Gafner
Herr Hans Peter Schläppi
Herr Zwahlen
and to those other members of the Lenk community who patiently listened to him and answered his questions.

He would also like to thank Herr Karl Fuchs (Senior), Herr Karl Fuchs (Junior) and Herr Hans Bishoff for their kindness in meeting him and supplying the information about Wengen that he required.

His thanks are also due to the Reverend Canon H.J. Hammerton and Herr Hans Bishoff for reading the script and especially to Monsieur Theodore Senn for his invaluable advice on the writing of the book.

And his especial thanks are due to the former Ambassador to Switzerland, Mr J R Rich C.M.G. for his extreme kindness in also writing a foreword to this his second book, and for the kind things he says in it.

EXPLANATION OF SWISS INSTITUTIONS

THE SWISS CONFEDERATION is a federation of 26 states called cantons, six of which rank as half cantons. These, in turn, are divided up into around 3,060 local authorities called communes.

THE SWISS PARLIAMENT comprises:

THE NATIONAL COUNCIL
(Representing the People)
THE STATES COUNCIL
(Representing the cantons)
} Together these form the FEDERAL ASSEMBLY

THE FEDERAL COUNCIL - the Cabinet or Government consisting of seven ministers elected by the Federal Assembly.

THE FEDERAL SUPREME COURT - the Judiciary situated in Lausanne.

THE SWISS NATIONAL BANK - a special statutory public limited company which controls the Swiss banking system.

SUVA - the Swiss Accident Insurance Association.

AHV - Insurance against Old Age and Bereavement, to provide pensions for the retired, widows and orphans.

UV - Accident Insurance.

IV - Disablement Insurance.

AV - Unemployment Insurance.

EO - Indemnity for the loss of earnings for militia.
men and civil defence recruits on being called up.

BVG - Occupational provision for Old-age, Disablement and Bereavement, to provide pensions for the retired, disabled, and widows and orphans - supplementary to AHV

9

VERNEHMLASSUNG - General Hearing. The opportunity given to interest groups, cantons and political parties to offer criticism and suggestions for improvement to a draft parliamentary bill.

SCHWEIZERISCHER FRAUENVEREIN - Swiss Women's Association, a national women's movement devoted to social work.

REFERENDUM - A general vote by the people.

INITIATIVE - The means whereby the people may initiate legislation.

The fact that certain titles and terms in this book are given in German and not in other languages spoken in Switzerland is no reflection upon the latter, but simply because the writer is more conversant with German. All these titles and terms, of course, have their equivalent in the other languages.

HISTORY OF THE SWISS CONFEDERATION

The Swiss Confederation was originally founded in 1291, when men of the cantons of Uri, Schwyz and Unterwalden met in the Rütli Meadow on the shores of Lake Lucerne and signed the Federal Letter.

Since 1291 the Swiss Confederation has had two distinct political forms. From 1291 to 1848 (apart for the five years of the Helvetic Republic, 1798 to 1803) it was a loose alliance of sovereign states known in German as a Staatenbund. In 1848 this Staatenbund was transformed into a federal state, in German a Bundesstaat, but it continued to be called the Swiss Confederation.

In order to differentiate between these two different political forms (Staatenbund and Bundesstaat) it is perhaps preferable to refer to the former as the old Swiss Confederation.

INTRODUCTION

Most people agree that there are two distinct parts to human make-up, namely a personal or individual aspect, and also a social or communal disposition. While on the one hand human beings are individuals who in order to be happy must follow their own personal inclinations and pursue their own individual objectives in order to establish a unique identity, they are, nevertheless gregarious creatures also requiring social contact with their fellows.

It is because they are social animals as well as individualists that they cannot act totally selfishly. They are obliged to come to terms with their fellows and work in partnership with them if society is to function and if they themselves are to be content. In addition there is undoubtedly a spiritual dimension to human beings which has engaged the attention of philosophers and religious thinkers throughout the ages, but one which the writer of this book is not competent to deal with. He will, therefore, confine his attention to people as individuals and social creatures.

These two fields of self interest and communal interest can, of course, overlap and come into conflict with each other. The freedom and rights of one individual are bounded by those of another, but friction between human beings is clearly reduced, even if not obviated, in proportion to the extent to which each individual adopts personally responsible attitudes towards his or her fellows. A balance must always be kept between self interest and duty towards one's neighbour. It is therefore imperative that those who are responsible for the ordering of society, those legislators whose duty it is to draw up state constitutions and make laws, should recognise these two areas of human make up, provide for them and define their limits as clearly as possible.

Any social or political system which acknowledges these two areas of a person's life and succeeds in creating a framework in which these natural requirements can be most fully satisfied, will be the one most conducive to human good and therefore the one also which is most likely to commend itself to the individual. It is only within such a framework that individuals are likely to achieve the required balance between personal gratification and social commitment which is necessary for their self fulfilment, satisfaction and thereby their contentment.

The Swiss social and political system is to a certain extent unique in that despite the many difficulties and setbacks which it has encountered during its long development through the ages, it can now claim, perhaps more than others, to be one which provides for the basic and natural requirements of its citizens to a large degree.

In that the Swiss Federal Constitution confers a large amount of personal freedom on the individual, it thereby offers him or her extensive opportunity for self development. At the same time it makes provision for his or her responsible participation and partnership in the running of the country's political and social life and creates a framework for satisfying their social needs as well. Within this framework the Swiss citizen is given both opportunity and encouragement to participate extensively in Swiss social and political life in partnership with his or her fellows.

That it has been possible for the Swiss, over the ages, to evolve such a social and political system is due, in a large part, to certain geographical, historical and economic factors which are peculiar to Switzerland. It is equally due to the fact that the Swiss people have proved themselves capable of learning and assimilating lessons from these factors and of translating and incorporating them into a social and political system, and also of being able to adopt and develop such mature social and political attitudes as to make the running of such a system possible.

The aim of this book will be to relate how this Swiss political and social system evolved and developed. As the hallmark of the system is the unique extent to which Swiss citizens collaborate with their fellows in the running of that system, the aim will also be to describe how that spirit of partnership originated and developed, and how it manifests itself today.

14

1

THE ORIGINS OF PARTNERSHIP

Environment has had an enduring effect on the outlook and attitudes of the Swiss people and on the ordering of their social and political institutions. Certain geographical factors have exerted an influence, not only upon the character and behaviour of the Swiss people, but also upon their activities and especially upon their economic outlook and policies.

Switzerland is a mountainous country with a harsh climate in those mountains in winter. Her land is, for the most part sparse and she possesses few natural resources. A further determining factor is the location of the country, because Switzerland lies at the crossroads of Europe, where some of the most important trade routes intersect and she has no direct access to the sea. It is these factors which have been largely responsible for the development of certain qualities of character and patterns of behaviour in the Swiss people - especially their adoption of attitudes of co-operation and partnership with one another.

Switzerland is a tiny country in the heart of Europe, largely mountainous and intersected by deep valleys. For many centuries, in winter when the snow was deep, the remote mountain areas were cut off from each other and from the valley below for long periods. Consequently, as no outside help could be expected if misfortune befell them, the people were compelled to rely on their own resources and upon one another. And as misfortune and misadventure are no respectors of persons, in that they strike both rich and poor alike, they have had a levelling effect on these communities as well.

The need to co-operate was strengthened by the fact that in Switzerland land available for cultivation is sparse. One quarter of the land is unproductive mountains and lakes, a second is woodland, a third quarter mostly alpine grazing land, with only the fourth quarter truly productive. Because there was so little fertile land in the mountainous areas a livelihood for everyone could only be provided if the inhabitants were prepared to join forces in performing the more laborious and onerous agricultural tasks in order to ensure that every available inch was cultivated. This could only be achieved if barren or remote areas were made fertile by irrigation, and this meant the ducting of water to them, sometimes for long distances. The construction and laying of these water-ducts required a combined effort of the men of the communities. What was true of irrigation was also true of the work in the forests, on the mountainsides and in the protection of the villages from avalanches and landslides and this may explain why even today more than two thirds of Switzerland's woodland is communally owned.

Because Switzerland has such a small area of genuinely productive land she has always had great difficulty in feeding her people. For centuries many Swiss had to seek employment abroad, mostly as mercenaries, but others as emigrants to the more prosperous parts of the earth. Nor has Switzerland ever had a surplus of raw materials which she could trade for supplementary food. In consequence the trade routes which crossed her territories assumed greater importance as a source of income. Only by using the monies derived from these European trade routes was Switzerland able to buy the extra provisions and later raw materials that she needed.

Just as the Swiss quickly learned that as individuals they could not live solely unto themselves, so they also quickly learned that collectively they were dependent on others. It was the realization of their dependence on the outside world which led to their adoption of realistic economic policies which would promote trade with other countries. The vital necessity to cultivate and maintain close economic links with foreign countries became an all-important guiding principle which has run right through Swiss history to the present day. It is one which the Swiss have always regarded of being of paramount importance to their welfare, and indeed, to their survival. Swiss history is the story of the efforts made by the Swiss to maintain these economic relationships with the outside world and to re-establish them, or create new ones, whenever they were broken.

When the Romans invaded central Switzerland in the second and first centuries BC certain Celtic tribes were already settled there. The most important of these were the Helvetii, who gave their name to the country Helvetia.

The trade routes through Switzerland apparently first came into prominence at the time of the Greeks and Etruscans, who bought their tin in Cornwall, in south-west England. The easiest way to procure the tin was to ship it to Greece through the Straits of Gibraltar and the Mediterranean. However the Carthaginians had complete control of the western Mediterranean so the Greek and Etruscan merchants chose the safer land routes across France and Switzerland. While this situation prevailed the Swiss prospered by offering transit and services to the Greek and Etruscan merchants who crossed their country. In 146 BC, however, Carthage was conquered by the Romans and the trade routes over the Alps declined in importance and trade through Switzerland diminished. This was of serious consequence to the Helvetii and they promptly took action to establish fresh commercial contacts with the outside world.

2

MASS EMIGRATION

The Helvetii twice decided to move their commercial base in order to get back into world trade. The first attempt to emigrate en masse to Gaul was made by one section of the Helvetii peoples in 107 BC, but they returned home almost immediately. A second mass emigration by more of the Helvetii followed in 58 BC. It proved to be a massive undertaking and three years were spent preparing for it. This preparation entailed widespread co-operation on the part of the Helvetii, so much so that it may perhaps be regarded as the first example of concerted Swiss endeavour. Provisions, supplies, equipment, draught animals and animals for slaughter were assembled and on 28 March 58 BC, 368,000 men, women and children set out from near Nyon for the promised land around Cognac in France. With them went an army of 90,000 men. Julius Caesar, on hearing of this exodus from Switzerland, hastened northwards from Rome with an army and defeated the Helvetii at the Battle of Bibracte. The Helvetii were, once again obliged to return home - only to find that their lands had been conquered by the Romans in their absence. The Romans were hated as invaders, but they achieved for the Helvetii what the mass emigrations had failed to do, namely the re-integration of Switzerland into international trade. The Romans built new roads over the Alps linking Switzerland with Rome thereby forging new links for the Swiss with the outside world.

During the period in which Greek and Etruscan

Merchants crossed their territory the Swiss came into close contact with Greek civilization. As a result of being incorporated in the Roman Empire they became closely involved in Roman civilization. Later still, as trade developed, Switzerland was able to cultivate close relations with the northern, eastern and western parts of Europe. This was especially so after she began to hire her sons out as mercenaries to the princely houses of Europe at the beginning of the 15th century and also after her universities became renowned as centres of learning in the later Middle Ages.

3

THE ALEMANNI

A Germanic tribe, the Alemanni invaded Switzerland in 260 AD, as the Roman Empire began to decline. Not a great deal is known about them. They do not appear to have been a homogeneous tribe, but rather a mixture of peoples who came together in the second century AD with the common objective of migrating south to find land where they could settle. They penetrated the Limes, the northern frontier of the Roman Empire, in 260 AD and by a series of thrusts forward gradually took possession of the whole of present-day eastern and central Switzerland.

At first they were feared by the Romans, but over a period of time they appear to have become more civilized and refined. It was they who assimulated the remants of the Roman people who were left in eastern and central Switzerland after the fall of the Roman Empire, into their culture. Whereas the other Germanic tribes who settled in Switzerland about this time, namely the Langobards in the south and the Burgundians in the west, adopted the culture and tradition of their host country, the Alemanni appear to have been able very largely to preserve their own culture, tradition, language and social organization, and to impose them widely on the indigenous peoples. These Alemannic attributes had an enduring effect on the Swiss people and on the development of Swiss political and social institutions.

The Alemanni were reputed to have had a pronounced love of freedom and a remarkable sense of social solidarity. They fully respected private property in the village communities, but at the same time they always retained certain land as common property to be cultivated and administered communally. Authority lay in the hands of the men who carried arms.

It was within these Alemanni communities that those co-operative forms of organization developed whose remnants still remain in the Swiss alpine areas in the form of Korporationen, Allmenden and Genossamen. The Alemanni communities also had a self-elected judicial system which has left its mark on the Swiss Federal legal system. In these communities a conscious middle class developed which was to prove of benefit to the later political development of the country. This middle class acted as a deterrent in the southern part of central Swizerland to the incursion of economic and political feudalism, when this was brought to Switzerland by the Franks and it provided material for a future ruling class which would be competent to take over authority when feudalism began to decline.

The Alemannic idea that political power should be broadly based by being vested in the people and not in an individual ruler or king was to be one of the basic tenets of a subsequent Swiss democratic creed, and later be incorporated in the Swiss Federal Constitution. To a large extent subsequent Swiss history is the story of the lengthy and gradual process of the putting into effect of these basic social and political conceptions which the Alemanni introduced into Switzerland.

Almost 16 centuries were to elapse before these political conceptions, sown by the Alemanni, were to be fully developed, incorporated into the Swiss Federal Constitution and translated into a permanent state structure. During this process of political development there were to be many set-backs. There were periods of progress followed by those of stagnation and even regression. But the tender democratic political plant which the Alemanni brought with them when they invaded Switzerland in the third century AD never withered completely, and after barren periods it always revived again and grew a little stronger.

4

THE FRANKS

The first real threat to the Alemanni and their political outlook and organization came from the Franks, another Germanic tribe who conquered the Burgundians in 534 AD and gradually took possession of the Alemanni territories during the next two centuries. When Charlemagne's empire was divided up in 870 AD, Burgundy was given to the West Franks and the Alemanni territories to the East Franks.

The Franks spread the feudal system, and serfdom throughout Europe and as a result, the disposal of the land and its products and the people who tilled the land largely passed into the hands of a bellicose nobility. In return for a grant of land these nobles were required to do military service for their king and to administer their territories. The landowners had an obligation to protect the peasants, but also the right to administer the law and levy taxes. This conception of feudalism with power in the hands of the Emperor and large land-owning families, and with the peasants subject to them, was a far cry from the old Alemannic idea of small self-governing communities with power in the hands of the people.

The introduction of the feudal system into Switzerland, with its rigid authority and control, was a backward step in the social and political development of the country, but the Alemannic tradition never seemed fully to have died out. The Alemannic middle class was allowed to retain a certain amount of independence by the Franks and over a period of time they developed their own aristocracy. The land conquered by the Franks included the southern part of central Switzerland, but because this area was remote from the centres of political power it appears to have been largely neglected by the Frankish rulers. As a result of this the Alemannic tradition of political freedom was able to be preserved in this area, and it was here that the modern Swiss Federal State was to have its birth.

Largely as a result of the feudal system, much of Europe stagnated economically during the 10th and 11th centuries and during this period the Swiss peasants lived from hand to mouth. The large landowning families, in their thirst for personal aggrandisement, waged war on each other and devastated the land; trade and industry deteriorated and the towns fell into decay.

As the years went by the size of the territories of many of the landowners diminished while their life-style became more lavish as a result of the new luxuries coming into Europe from Byzantium and the Arab world. It became increasingly more difficult for them to make both ends meet, but they were helped by a revival in Swiss agriculture during the 12th and 13th centuries which resulted from the introduction of new farming methods.

This revival in agriculture co-incided with an upsurge in trade and industry in the towns, after the Muslims, who had occupied the Mediterranean basin since the 7th century, had been driven back.

In order to supplement their income the old aristocratic landowners were compelled to lease their lands to tenant farmers, to sell rights and priviledges to merchants and patrician families in the towns and also to sell the right to found new towns. As the tenant farmers prospered they became more and more independent of their landlords and as trade and commerce flourished in the towns and when new towns were built, the merchant and patrician families were gradually able to throw off the yoke of their former hereditary rulers. In both the towns and on the land, a new propertied class developed which, with the remnants of the old Alemannic aristocracy, was able to assume authority as the power of the old landowning families waned. Of the old large landowning families that still remained in Switzerland at the end of the 13th century, the most prominent were the House of Savoy in western Switzerland and the Habsburg family in central and eastern Switzerland.

This gradual transfer of power from the old aristocratic landowning families and with it the demise of feudalism and serfdom, marked a significant step forward in Swiss political development. From now on political authority, in both the towns and the valley communities, was to become more broadly based. This did not represent an immediate progression to democracy as we know it today, because the franchize in these units was still very limited. Nevertheless, it did represent a marked political advance, because from now on both the towns and the valley communities were to be ruled by elected assemblies instead of by one powerful aristocratic ruler and his subordinates. Because the hereditary ruling families were often no longer able to preserve law and order in their territories, the town and valley communities now began to conclude alliances between themselves in order to ensure peaceful conditions.

Probably because there were no important trade routes crossing the Alps from north to south in central Switzerland, for centuries, this part of the country remained a backwater. The interest of the hereditary ruling powers seems to have been concentrated, during this period, on other parts of Switzerland, but towards central Switzerland they appear to have pursued a policy of benign neglect. The result was that the area around Lake Lucerne remained remote from their authority and administration, and particularly the area at the southern end of the lake at the foot of the St. Gotthard Pass. Whether it was solely because of this neglect, or whether the people living in these valleys had an earlier success in obtaining their freedom from their hereditary overlords by obtaining the privilege from the Emperor of coming under his direct suzerainty, or whether in this part of the world the Alemannic tradition had been more fully preserved, we do not know: what is certain is that in this area, by the beginning of the 13th century, there were valley communities which were largely independent of their feudal overlords. Among these were the people of

Uri who lived at the foot of the St. Gotthard Pass.

The attitude of the hereditary landlords and that of the Imperial authorities changed towards this area when the men of Uri succeeded in building a new bridge over the River Reuss in the wild Schöllenen ravine, around 1240, and so made the St. Gotthard route the shortest link between Italy and northern Europe. The St. Gotthard Pass immediately assumed tremendous importance for the Habsburgs as a line of communication. In the next 50 years trade over the pass increased greatly and the people of the cantons around Lake Lucerne prospered as a result. They were loth to surrender control over the route and this brought them into direct conflict with their landlords and the representatives of the Holy Roman Empire of which their territories formed part.

5

THE BIRTH OF FEDERALISM

Ostensibly to safeguard their independence and the rights and privileges which they enjoyed, and which they believed their hereditary rulers were no longer in a position to ensure for them, the men of the cantons of Uri, Schwyz and Unterwalden met in the first days of August, 1291, in the Rütli meadow overlooking Lake Lucerne and concluded or re-affirmed a collective security agreement. This is known as the Federal Letter and has been preserved to this day.

In reality, however, this undertaking by the men of Uri, Schwyz and Unterwalden to exclude the representatives of their feudal overlords from their lands was prompted basically by commercial motives, namely to retain in their own hands the control of the St Gotthard route, and the revenues which accrued from it. By so doing they were merely obeying the age-old economic imperative to maintain and develop trade relations with the outside world in order to survive. The oath sworn in the Rütli meadow was to prove to be more than just a mutual defence pact. It was to assume historical significance in that it proved to be the founding act of the Swiss National State.

The valley communities and the burghers of the towns were quick to seize any opportunity offered to them to acquire their freedom from their hereditary overlords, and as these merchant families prospered, they became more than a match for their former rulers. By purchasing land, rights and privileges from the latter they gradually consolidated their proprietorship and authority, not only

26

in the towns themselves, but also over large areas of the surrounding land. Bern, Zurich and Basel serve as typical examples of this policy of land acquisition.

With the decline of the old traditional ruling houses, the peoples of central Switzerland lost their former protecting powers, and from now on were compelled to protect themselves. They were especially anxious to safeguard their newly-acquired rights, the towns and bridges within their territories, and to obviate internal strife and family feuds. To this end these new self-governing town and valley communities began to conclude defence treaties with each other. Political necessity compelled them to co-operate for a common purpose and although these alliances were imperfect and changed frequently, they were the basis of Swiss federalism. From then on a loose political structure began to take shape, which gradually over a period of about 600 years would develop into a national state.

The conclusion of defence alliances between town and valley communities was made even more necessary by the reaction of the Habsburgs to the oath sworn by the men of Uri, Schwyz and Unterwalden to exclude foreign magistrates from their lands. This was a direct challenge to Habsburg authority and they could not regard it with indifference because the revenue to be derived from the St Gotthard trade route was too great to be given up. Neither did they want to have the old Alemannic concept of sovereignty of the people put into effect in the very heart of their territories.

The Habsburgs were fully determined to bring the St Gotthard Pass under their control and in order to accomplish this they sent an Austrian army to block it. For the Swiss Confederates it was a matter of economic and political life and death that it should remain in their hands, so they called in the help of the people of Zurich by signing a treaty with them.

The struggle for liberation from the Habsburgs which followed is immortalised in the William Tell saga. How much of this is fact and how much is fiction is difficult to determine. There is no doubt that William Tell does personify the struggle of the Swiss to free themselves from the yoke of their feudal overlords and oppressors. What is certain is that the alliance formed between the cantons of Uri, Schwyz and Unterwalden, in 1291, was joined by Lucerne in 1332, Zurich in 1351 and Bern in 1353. Bit by bit the Confederates freed themselves from the Habsburg yoke. By the peaceful purchase of rights and territories, and by waging war, they succeeded in extending their lands, and the battles of Sempach in 1386 and Näfels in 1388 proved decisive victories for them in their struggle.

During the second half of the 14th century not only was the political authority of the Habsburgs broken in central Switzerland, but also that of the new landed class who ruled in the rural areas. Their land, and their taxes and juridicial rights were communalised. In these rural areas political authority was now vested in Landsgemeinden or public assemblies, where decisions were taken democratically. In the towns too, democratic development took a futher step forward in that political authority became vested, more and more in the guilds and merchant families.

The Confederates agreed to two more pacts between themselves, namely the Pfaffen Letter and the Sempach Letter in which they undertook to administer the Law themselves in all the territories under their control, to ensure internal peace, and to enforce disipline in all future military ventures. Although, as has been said, these treaties which the cantons entered into were loose arrangements, by the end of the 14th century a confederation of independent Swiss localities was taking shape within the Holy Roman Empire. Another 100 years were to elapse before the final fetters of the Holy Roman Empire were thrown off. This was accomplished at the Battle of Dornach in 1499 in which the Austrians were decisively defeated. Full acknowledgement of the situation was not forthcoming until the end of the Thirty Years War in 1648, when the existence of a confederation of Swiss states was recognized and written down in the Treaty of Westphalia.

In the meantime the Swiss Confederates, and especially those in the towns, flushed by their early successes against the Habsburgs, embarked on military campaigns in order to extend their territories, and a century of territorial expansion followed.

In order to secure the southern approaches to the St Gotthard Pass, the Urner and the men of Obwalden invaded the Ticino. An uprising in St Gallen town against the Abbot of St Gallen, and one in canton Appenzell provided excuses for the Confederates to intervene in these disputes and thereby extend their land northwards. A quarrel between the Habsburgs and the Emperor of the Holy Roman Empire, Sigismund of Luxemburg, also gave the Confederates the excuse for intervention and enabled them to annex the Aargau as a vassal territory.

The Confederates also turned their attention westwards to where Charles the Bold, Duke of Burgundy, was blocking their access to French and Spanish markets. This thrust westwards was spearheaded by Bern. The Bernese defeated Charles the Bold at the Battle of Murten in 1476, and the Duke himself died a year later. The Bernese now had the upper hand and they even advanced to the gates of Geneva. Finally the canton of Vaud was brought to submission in 1536 and made a vassal state. As a result of these campaigns the Bernese gained their objectives fully for the way now lay open for trade with Geneva, Lyons, Spain and the newly-found colonies overseas.

In the north of Switzerland the Confederates, under the leadership of Zurich, became embroiled in a war with the Swabian League as a result of which they gained complete jurisdiction over the Thurgau. But the territorial gains which the Confederates had to show from all these military campaigns were not spectacular, because they often lacked unified action and purpose. Rivalries between the cantons became even more pronounced as the power of the Habsburgs waned, because conflicts of interest in the territories ceded by the Habsburgs increased. Bern clashed with Fribourg and Lucerne, Zurich with Schaffhausen, and after the death of the last Count of Toggenburg in 1436, Zurich and Schwyz waged a ten-year war over the inheritance. The lesson of effective political co-operation had still to be learned by the Swiss Confederates.

In addition, certain areas that the Confederates had conquered, such as the Aargau, Thurgau and areas around Sargans and south of the Gotthard became vassal territories and were administered jointly by the cantons which led to continual friction. In order to reduce difficulties and misunderstandings between the cantons, a joint assembly was set up to administer the vassal territories which would consist of two representatives from each canton. This assembly, known as the Tagsatzung, was the first political organ of a slowly emerging Swiss federal state, and it was to remain operative, if not outstandingly effective, for the next 300 years. Here again, it was political necessity which prompted the initiation of an embryonic federal political structure in Switzerland.

The internal rivalries which developed during this period were not solely between the towns which as they expanded outwards, created vassal territories of their own in the surrounding rural areas which they exploited. The inhabitants of these rural areas resented the attempts of such towns as Zurich and Bern to police and administer their territories, take over the old feudal taxes and dues, and to abrogate their rights.

To this resentment towards the towns was added the bad feeling which the peasants harboured as a result of the practice of hiring mercenaries out to foreign powers. It is true that the country was so poor that many Swiss youths had no alternative other than to enlist for military service in foreign armies, but these mercenaries resented the method by which they were recruited - namely that the ruling families in the town and rural cantons sold the right to enlist them in their territories to the princely houses of Europe and became extremely rich by so doing. The peasants, naturally, resented having to spill their blood in order to enrich their oppressive rulers, and they rose up against them. The towns grew fearful of revolution and formed a defensive alliance which did nothing to allay the fears and resentment of the peasants. There were continual uprisings by the peasants and these were cruelly suppressed.

In 1481, an all-out civil war seemed imminent, but fortunately a certain Niklaus von Flüh of Einsiedeln intervened, called the dissidents and their oppressors together; and a compromise formula was worked out in the Stans Agreement. Even so, in 1513, there were renewed revolts in Bern, Lucerne and Solothurn against the shameless enriching of partrician families through the sale of mercenaries.

The most acute crisis in the sale of mercenaries came during the Italian wars around Milan in the late 15th and early 16th centuries. In conflict were the Dukes of Milan and the French and Papal forces, and it was found that Swiss mercenaries had been hired by both sides and were fighting each other.

The old Swiss Confederation was also engaged in these wars, first on the side of the French and later against them. This was to prove to be the last Swiss military campaign fought under the Swiss flag outside Switzerland, other than a short foray during the Hundred Days at the end of the Napoleonic Wars. At the Battle of Marignano in 1515, the Swiss were confronted by a reorganised French army and from it they encountered concentrated musketry fire for the first time. They were so heavily defeated by the French that they abandoned their policy of aggrandisement for ever, withdrew into their own territories and adopted a policy of neutrality. It was a most important decision on the part of the Swiss Confederates and it was to have a considerable effect on the development of their country. Peace was concluded with France in 1516 and later in 1521, France was given the exclusive right to levy mercenaries throughout Switzerland with the exception of Zurich. This treaty with France lasted almost 200 years and it formed the basis of close military and economic co-operation between the two countries.

The defeat of the Swiss Confederates at the Battle of Marignano was a blessing in disguise, for it taught them that aggression, in the long run, is unrewarding and that co-operation with one's neighbour is more likely to promote national well-being than is confrontation. But much Swiss blood had still to be shed in religious wars and civil strife before the lessons of non-aggression and tolerance within the country were accepted.

6

THE COMING OF CHRISTIANITY

The earliest Christian inscriptions in Switzerland were found in canton Valais and date back to 377 AD. By the beginning of the 5th century AD a very active Christian cult was being practised around St Mauritius, who is reputed to have suffered martydom near St Maurice with his Theban Legion around 290 AD for having manifested his Christian faith.

A second Christian missionary thrust into Switzerland came from the monastic house of Condate in the Jura in the 5th century. By the next century there would appear to have been numerous Christian churches scattered along the northern shore of Lake Geneva and the Christianization of Graubünden also appears to have taken place at an early date.

A widespread conversion of Switzerland to Christianity, however, was only effected much later by the Franks. The impetus for this movement stemmed from the Irish monks of the monastery of Luxeuil in the Vosges Mountains, which had been founded towards the end of the 6th century. Christianity seems to have spread only slowly throughout the country, but as it spread monasteries and religious houses were built which became centres of culture and learning.

The most famous of these Swiss monasteries in the Middle Ages were the religious houses of St Gallen in the north of the country, and St Maurice in the south-west. The influence of both spread far beyond the frontiers of Switzerland.

The uniting of the country in a single faith provided the basis for a Swiss national state. Although a major schism occurred in the Church in the 16th century, by that time Christian faith and teaching had become so firmly rooted that the Swiss people were able to withstand the organizational disruption of the Reformation and come to terms with it.

7

THE REFORMATION

The Reformation in Switzerland was not merely a protest by Protestant reformers against abuses in the Roman Catholic Church - it had a political connotation also. It began in Zurich when Ulrich Zwingli came to the Great Minster as lay priest in 1518. Zwingli's religious views were influenced by Luther. He called for the reinstitution of the authority of the Bible, condemned the laxity of the Roman priesthood, and opposed pluralism and the sale of Indulgences. Politically he opposed the worldliness of the Roman Catholic Church and condemned its earthly possessions. He won support in the rural cantons by denouncing serfdom and that of the guilds in Zurich by condemning the trade in mercenaries.

In 1525, the Zurich town council adopted his teachings and seized the possessions of the Roman Catholic Church in Zurich and its surrounding areas. Other town authorities quickly followed suit and as a result of acquiring valuable church property greatly increased their power. But many of them abused their newly-acquired authority by imposing heavy tax burdens on the vassal territories by which they were surrounded. In consequence the people in the rural areas once again revolted and were once again cruelly suppressed and made completely subject to the towns.

The Reformation spread rapidly and wherever it took root it increased the power of the towns over rural areas. The central areas of Switzerland, however, remained largely faithful to the Roman Catholic Church, and towns such as Lucerne and Zug and some rural cantons, now fearful of the increasing power of the Protestant towns, and the threat that this posed to their freedom, decided in 1524 to conclude a mutual alliance.

Zwingli now worked out plans whereby the towns of Zurich and Bern were to be given full authority in the old Swiss Confederation and the rural cantons were to be excluded from participation in the administration. This was resented by the rural areas and tension grew. Breaking point came over a religious difference in the Aargau and war broke out between the Protestant towns and the Catholic cantons in 1529.

There were two wars, known as the First and Second Kappel Wars (1529 and 1531). Zwingli was killed in the 1531 conflict. The issue was finally decided in favour of the Catholics, and as a result, for almost 200 years, a Catholic minority exercised political authority over a Protestant majority in the old Swiss Confederation.

In western Switzerland the Reformation was not just a matter of religious confrontation between Protestantism and Catholicism - it was also a political conflict. Whereas in northern Switzerland the power of the hereditary aristocratic powers had already been largely broken by the time the Reformation broke out, in the French-speaking part the House of Savoy still held authority in Geneva and over large parts of canton Vaud. Both Bern and Fribourg had treaties with Geneva, but whereas Bern had adopted Protestantism, Fribourg had remained true to the old faith. Geneva had to choose between them and she opted for Protestantism. With the help of Bern she freed herself from the shackles of the House of Savoy. In 1536 Calvin came to Geneva and in the same year Bern took possession of many of those territories in canton Vaud which had formerly belonged to the House of Savoy.

The old Swiss Confederation was now split into two religious groups or alliances, one Protestant and one Catholic. The Protestants outnumbered the Catholics by two to one, and the Reformers also held most of the important commercial centres. The Zwinglian and Calvinist towns issued a joint declaration of faith, the

'Confessio Helvetia posterior'. Their antagonism to the Imperial Catholic territories bordering on Switzerland, which were allied to their Catholic opponents, gradually led to the secession of the old Swiss Confederation from the Holy Roman Empire.

The Swiss Catholics, grouped together in the Swiss Catholic League, continued to maintain contact with Catholic countries outside Switzerland and especially with Spain. There were tremendous religious tensions in Switzerland at this time, especially in those vassal territories jointly administered by cantons professing different faiths, but loyalty to this common administration and joint endeavour prevailed over the disruptive tendencies of religious difference. Cohesion was preserved because a Swiss national consciousness was slowly developing which was to stand proof against all subsequent disruptive political and religious forces.

The dominant position of the towns was also strengthened at this time by an influx of refugees fleeing from religious persecution abroad. The wool, linen, silk, watch-making and banking industries received a tremendous stimulus from these refugees, and in addition they helped to spread industry from the towns into the surrounding rural areas, mostly in the form of home industry. The increase in prosperity which followed the arrival of these refugees increased the power of the ruling patrician families. By hiring out mercenaries, acquiring land and participating in trade and industry, these families had become rich and politically powerful, but history was to repeat itself. Just as the old aristocratic families had become conservatively rigid in their attitudes, so now did this new ruling class. It allowed no newcomers to participate in the joint endeavour of cultivating common land, and it restricted participation in the administration of town and country cantons. Autonomy was taken from the rural areas surrounding the towns and the people in these areas were submitted to the oppressive jurisdiction of this new urban ruling class.

In 1653 the peasants of the cantons of Lucerne, Bern, Solothurn and Basel met in Huttwil, formed an alliance and the Peasants' War broke out. This peasants' uprising, like the ones that had preceded it, was ruthlessly suppressed. The ringleaders were hanged, tortured or proscribed; all rights and privileges were withdrawn from them, and crippling fines imposed on them. The new ruling aristocracy in the towns had acquired complete power.

Zurich now attempted to reform the constitution of the old Swiss Confederation to the advantage of the towns and to Zurich and Bern in particular, but such was the opposition from the rural cantons that the attempt came to nothing. Civil war broke out and at the Battle of Villmergen in 1656, Protestant Bern lost 500 killed. As a result of this victory the Catholic cantons gained a predominant influence which lasted for a futher 56 years. But it was an uneasy peace. Religious disputes arose continuously and arbiters had to be called in continually to mediate. These arbiters were usually Catholics and not always impartial in their findings. Friction continued and war broke out again. At the second Battle of Villmergen in 1712 the issue was settled in favour of the Protestant towns and the Catholic supremacy in the jointly administered vassal territories was broken. The Catholics were excluded from condominium in Baden and all religious disputes were now to be settled by a commission consisting of an equal number of Protestant and Catholic members. As a result of this settlement religious strife began to subside after almost 200 years. The Swiss Confederates were slowly learning to be tolerant.

The political situation in Switzerland remained almost unchanged until Napoleon invaded the country in 1797. The towns, ruled by a rigid, oppressive, but decreasing aristocracy, retained their ascendancy in the old Swiss Confederation, and they vigorously suppressed any attempts at insurrection on the part of the people.

But during the second half of the 18th century there was change and development in other areas. Improved methods of farming greatly contributed to an increased yield of agricultural produce. An extension of home industry in the textile and watch-making industries increased output to such an extent that by the end of the century Switzerland had become the most industrialized country on the Continent.

The greatest development, however, was in the field of ideas; in political and social thinking. Enlightened thinkers and citizens were no longer content to be excluded from political decision-making, and as the ordinary people became more and more disillusioned with their oppressive rulers, they too called for basic human rights and an alleviation of the tax burden. The ideas of the Enlightenment, which culminated in the French Revolution, began to take firm root in Switzerland and Rationalism began to assert itself, especially in the economic field. Rigidly held religious positions began to soften or be replaced by more liberal conceptions and attitudes. To all this metamorphosis of ideas was added an upsurge in Swiss nationalist fervour and aspirations towards national unification.

The first struggles for constitutional changes came in Geneva between 1704 and 1707. In 1737, the first opponent of the patrician political hierarchy in the town achieved a political breakthrough. But despite the ever-decreasing number of patricians, it was not until 1782 that any significant number of Geneva citizens became enfranchised. In Bern and Zurich similar political struggles took place in order to secure political emancipation for the ordinary citizen, and in the process several dissidents were hanged by the aristocrats who clung to their political privileges to the bitter end. It is estimated that in the 18th century, prior to Napoleon's invasion, fewer than 200,000 people had access to political power in Switzerland, whereas the rest, more than a million inhabitants, played no part in government.

8

THE ADVENT OF NAPOLEON

The Swiss were able to steer clear of Napoleon's early
military campaigns, but after he conquered Italy, the
Swiss mountain passes became of considerable strategic
military importance to him as lines of communication
between Milan and Paris. He decided to take control of
the country. He took possession of the Bishopric of Basel
in 1797/1798 and then went on to occupy the whole of
Switzerland. Only Bern offered him any serious
resistance, but her armies were quickly defeated at the
Battle of Grauholz and the French occupied the town.

For the most part the ordinary Swiss citizens welcomed
Napoleon as a liberator from their patrician oppressors.
The ruling classes accepted the situation with as good a
grace as possible, but even so they had difficulty in
coming to terms with it. So once again the Swiss people
became free of aristocratic oppression, but in this case
only by accepting the occupation of the country by a
foreign power. Their emancipation was not to last for
long, because a partial return to the old régime was to
follow. Permanent emancipation was not to come until
1848.

The Helvetic Republic

After his occupation of the country in 1798, Napoleon
decided that Switzerland should have a completely new
constitution and state-form, similar to that of the French.
He created the Helvetic Republic, and for the first time

Switzerland became a political entity in Europe. The old Confederation of independent squabbling states was welded into one unit and overall political authority was vested centrally. The first paragraph of the Constitution of the Helvetic Republic runs: 'The Helvetic Republic constitutes one unified, undivided state. Boundaries between cantons and vassal territories no longer exist, nor do those between individual cantons'. The cantons were reorganized and deprived of their autonomy.

The Helvetic Republic recognised the sovereignty of the people within a centralised, democratic and representative form of state. It postulated basic human rights and civic rights were extended to all citizens, but in return those citizens were required to swear an oath of allegiance to the new constitution.

In the Constitution of the Helvetic Republic a separation of political authority was introduced. The Legislature, Executive and Judiciary were made completely distinct from each other in order to ensure independence and democratic control to these state institutions. The cantons had a purely administrative function but no real power.

Outlines of the subsequent legislative, executive and judiciary systems of the Swiss Federal State of 1848 are recognisable in their equivalents in the Helvetic Republic Constitution.

The Legislature was to consist of a Senate, to be composed of four deputies from each canton and former directors, and a Great Council consisting of eight members from each canton. This was later revised so that the number of representatives was proportioned to the size of the population. The Executive was to be called the Directory and consist of five members to be elected by the joint Houses of Parliament, but by a complicated electoral system. The Judiciary was to be composed of a supreme court and cantonal courts and this would also seem to have set a pattern for the Judiciary after 1848.

An outstanding difference, however, between the Helvetic Republic and the Swiss Confederation of 1848 was that whereas in the Helvetic Republic the cantons were directed and controlled by a Governor nominated by the Directory, in the Federal State after 1848, they were largely free to run their own affairs.

Napoleon also granted freedom to the press in the Helvetic Republic but this had to be withdrawn because of the criticism which this free press levelled at the Republic and a press censorship was then imposed.

Thus in many ways the Helvetic Republic was a forerunner of the 1848 Swiss Federal State.

Although the Helveltic Republic had only a short life its political effects were enduring. The unification of weights, measures, currency, the law and armed forces proved to be a subject of political discussion in Switzerland for the next 50 years, and the strict separation of Church from State was to have an effect on future legislation.

The Constitution of the Helvetic Republic was, perhaps, most far-reaching in the field of education. It maintained that it was the duty of an enlightened state to give its citizens an education worthy of their freedom. This showed a firm belief that man is capable of improvement, and that every educated person would accept inevitably the tenets of the Revolution and this prompted the authors of the Constitution of the Helvetic Republic to give an extension of education absolute priority. Although all the envisaged reforms were not effected during the lifetime of the Republic, they nevertheless proved to be a stimulus for future educational legislators.

The Helvetic Republic dismantled all the administrative structures of the old régime, but had great difficulty in replacing them with new ones. New structures were required for the administration, education, the law, the tax-system, the army and for those functions which the cantons and churches had formerly performed. It was decided that the old feudal tithes and taxes should be abolished, but there was a conflict of opinion on how they should be replaced by a universal tax. The Helvetic Republic therefore became a state short of money and without funds it is difficult for any state to function. At the same time the treasuries of the town cantons, which the patrician rulers had so painstakingly built up over the years, were depleted in order to buy the country's freedom from the French occupation. But parallel with the dismantling of the feudal system, a modern economic system was introduced which set a pattern for economic development in the future.

The Helvetic Republic soon came to be a battleground for internecine warfare between the Unitarians who favoured a unified state, and the Federalists, or conservatives, who supported a reversion to the former sovereignty of the cantons. First one party held power and then the other, so that when the French forces withdrew from Switzerland civil war broke out between them.

This gave Napoleon the excuse to invade Switzerland again in 1803 and impose an amended constitution on the country. This new constitution known as the 'Mediation', incorporated the vassal territories of Aargau, Thurgau, Ticino and Vaud and the allied territories of Graubünden and St Gallen in the old Swiss Confederation. Under it also the cantons regained many rights, because where under the Constitution of the Helvetic Republic a maximum amount of power had been vested in the central authority, the new Mediation Constitution restricted that power to an absolute minimum. Its commitments consisted merely of foreign policy, the army, customs dues and the authority to act as arbiter in cantonal disputes.

In the former Landsgemeinde cantons the original political situation was more or less restored. In the new cantons representative democracy was introduced, while in the town cantons the old patrician families largely regained power at the expense of the ordinary citizen. In this way a compromise was effected between Unitarians and Federalists. Certain individual freedoms acquired under the Helvetic Republic were retained and the Mediation restored federalism to Switzerland. As time went on it became obvious that the only permanent solution to the country's constitutional problem lay in a compromise between cantonal political authority and that of a Federal State, in other words, in a partnership between a Federal State and the cantons.

But the period of the Mediation did bring positive benefits to the country. It was during this period of relative calm that industry began to become concentrated in factories with the result that home industry began to decline. Perhaps the most effective political gain during this time was a reconciliation between the old aristocracy and the new social élite which had been created by trade and industry, because these two were to form a new governing class in the 19th century. The unifying factors between the groups were, firstly a common interest in opposing disruption, and secondly, the cultivation of a common intellectual outlook which laid great stress on Swiss traditional custom and usage and thereby on patriotism.

This situation lasted as long as Napoleon remained in power, but after he fell a reversion to the old order followed. Since 1798 too much had happened politically for the clock to be put back completely, but nevertheless, in 1815 a loose confederation of states was set up again in Switzerland, the aristocrats largely recovered their political authority and certain individual rights which the people had enjoyed under Napoleon were withdrawn.

9

1815 TO 1848

During the first half of the 19th century constitutional reform became a serious preoccupation of the cantons because liberal ideas could not be suppressed. Already before 1830 demands for personal freedom, basic human rights and representative democracy were being strongly urged in the cantonal parliaments, with the result that between 1830 and 1833 ten cantons had to amend their constitutions.

After 1830 the Regeneration movement set in. By means of petitions and the holding of public meetings it became possible to overthrow the aristocrats in many cantonal governments and here again new constitutions had to be drawn up which guaranteed civic rights to the people and the right to elect their representatives. In Basel the Regeneration movement led to civil war between the town and rural parts of the canton and this resulted in the splitting of the Basel Canton into two half cantons.

However all attempts to revise the Federal Constitution of 1815 failed and in Zurich and Lucerne the Conservatives even succeeded in ejecting the Radicals or Liberal Unitarians from cantonal government. The battle between those who wished to preserve the authority of the cantons and those who demanded a national state was fully joined.

The advance of Liberalism could not be halted. After 1830 a series of political struggles, and even military skirmishes, took place in the cantons. A movement from the people grew steadily which opposed the arbitrary rule of the aristocrats and the privileges of the Church. It called for freely elected parliaments in both Federal State and cantons and the guaranteeing of basic human rights.

To these political arguments for freedom and democracy from the people were added the economic arguments of the Liberals and Radicals. They demanded a unified economic trading area - in other words a national state - and the unification of weights and measures, currency and customs dues, in order to promote trade and industry.

The conservative ruling class was opposed to this political reform and fought bitterly against it. The Catholic cantons of central Switzerland called the Jesuits to Lucerne and formed a military alliance called the Sonderbund and were even prepared to ally with foreign powers to further their cause. The Liberal-Radicals were appalled by this and took determined counter-action.

In the Tagsatzung, the parliament of the old Swiss Confederation, the Liberal-Radicals now had 12 full and two half votes out of the 22 seats and so were in a position to commission General Dufour to suppress the uprising in Lucerne. After a short campaign he occupied the town, and the canton of Valais was the last member of the Sonderbund Alliance to surrender on 12 September 1848.

The campaign of General Dufour against the Sonderbund in 1848 was waged in a spirit of moderation and tolerance. His aim was not to annihilate or humiliate his opponents but to finish the campaign as quickly as possible with as few casualties as possible. That he was able to effect this within four weeks, with slightly more than 100 killed on both sides, is a tribute to his military expertise, magnanimity and moderation. As a result of this campaign he became a national hero.

His magnanimity and toleration were also to be reflected in the new Federal Constitution which was immediately drawn up when the campaign ended. Because in that this Federal Constitution of 1848 showed a spirit of moderation, tolerance and conciliation it set the stage and provided the climate for future co-operation and partnership between Swiss people.

For 550 years, apart for the short period of the Helvetic Republic, the old Swiss Confederation had been a loose alliance of small independent states. Now, by ratifying the new constitution, the Swiss took the step towards becoming a federal state.

10

THE SWISS FEDERAL CONSTITUTION

OF 1848

The Swiss Federal Constitution of 1848 recognized three political entities - the Federal State, the cantons and the people. This constitution created a free, constitutional, democratic Swiss Federal State. In it the Legislature was to consist of two chambers to be elected democratically by the people, namely, the National Council representing the people, and the States Council representing the cantons. Together these two chambers were to form the Federal Assembly which would be responsible for the election of seven councillors to the Federal Council which was to be the Government or Executive.

The Constitution of 1848 created a federal state out of a group of hitherto loosely allied independent cantons. These cantons surrended a part of their sovereignty to the new authority, but at the same time retained a large degree of autonomy in certain fields. The relationship between individual cantons and that between the cantons and the Federal State was institutionalised and defined. Provision was made for these conditions of relationship to be revised if necessary, at a later date, by means of a referendum of the people and cantons.

The compilers of the 1848 Constitution had the unenviable task of attempting to reconcile two conflicting political trends in Swiss 19th century politics, namely that of the progressive Liberal school, which sought a unified trading area and thereby a centralized state, and the

Catholic-Conservative faction which wished to retain cantonal sovereignty. The Constitution was an adroit compromise. The Progressives were satisfied in that a central authority in the form of the Swiss Federal State was created and that certain commitments, such as foreign relations and the supervision of the army, became its exclusive preserve, and also in that a unified trading area was created.

At the same time the Catholic-Conservatives were happy in that the cantons were able to retain a large amount of their autonomy. All those commitments which were not specifically assigned to the Federal State remained within their jurisdiction and they continued to be independent in many areas. The small Catholic rural cantons were especially happy that in the newly-formed States Council the full cantons were to have two votes and the half cantons one vote, irrespective of their size. This meant that a small canton such as Uri had as much say as Zurich, which was many times bigger. This concession on the part of the Liberal-Radicals, who drew up the constitution, was extremely magnanimous and far-sighted. It helped to calm the contentious political factions in the country and paved the way for reconciliation and the undertaking of joint commercial enterprises in the future.

With the defeat of the Catholics in the Sonderbund War and the introduction of a new constitution, power in Parliament had passed to the Liberal-Radicals and until 1891 they alone formed the Government.

The majority of these Liberal-Radicals had their origin in home industry in the countryside where they acted as middlemen between the industrialists in the towns and the handworkers on the land. As industry developed they became exceedingly powerful and like their aristocratic and patrician predecessors, they strove to monopolise economic and political power and retain both as a restricted preserve for themselves, their families and their friends. They had tremendous economic success. They were largely responsible for the building of the Swiss railways and for the banks which financed their construction, and for the mechanisation of the textile industry. These projects attracted capital, not only from the old patrician families, but also from this new and prosperous middle class which the reorganization and development of industry was creating.

The Liberal-Radical monoply of political power quickly created opponents, among them under-privileged hand and farm workers, democratic intellectuals, and former aristocratic and conservative federalists. An extreme left-wing movement, which was the forerunner of Socialism in Switzerland, made joint cause, albeit loosely, with extreme Conservatives who were predominantly federalists, to overthrow the Liberal-Radicals who were supporters of strong central government. These opponents of the Liberal-Radical government called for constitutional reform which would give greater democratic participation in government, for the creation of cantonal banks, in order to make credit available for the lower classes, for free education, lower taxes, and for better working conditions in the factories.

As on previous occasions, the movement for political reform began in the cantons, starting in Basel and spreading eastwards. In 1869 in Zurich the Democrats won power and from then on Zurich town council was elected democratically by the people - only men were enfranchised - and all subsequent laws enacted by the Zurich town council were made subject to a referendum. The Democrats' successful campaign was not to be halted. More democratic procedures spread from canton to canton until a revision of the Federal Constitution became inevitable, the more so because the Liberals themselves were also now in favour of reform in order to unify the army and commercial law. A new constitution was brought into force in 1874.

11

THE SWISS FEDERAL CONSTITUTION

OF 1874

For the most part, in the revision of the Federal Constitution in 1874 the basic elements of the Federal Constitution of 1848 were retained, but the process of making Switzerland into a free unified trading area was completed, the Swiss legal system made uniform, and the Swiss military system more or less unified.

The most significant innovation was the introduction of the Facultative or Optional Referendum, whereby 30,000 enfranchised citizens, later extended to 50,000, were given the right to demand a referendum on certain laws passed by the Federal Parliament, if they so wished. Eight cantons, acting together, were given the same right.

The introduction of the Facultative Referendum had a profound effect, because as a result of it political sovereignty passed from Parliament to the people, thus making Switzerland much more democratic. This democratic process was further developed in 1891, when the Peoples' Initiative was introduced which gave the right to 50,000 enfranchised citizens, later extended to 100,000, to propose legislation to the Federal Council, of which the latter was compelled to take notice.

This democratic process progressed still further when the proportional representation voting system was introduced in 1918 for elections to the National Council. It reached its culmination at national level in 1971, when the franchise was extended to include women.

As a result of all these measures political sovereignty became firmly vested in the Swiss people and a political partnership between people and Parliament established.

The revision of the Federal Constitution in 1874 spelled the end of a Liberal monopoly of power in the Swiss Parliament, because in that it gave an opportunity to the people to challenge the lawmakers, by allowing new laws to be submitted to a referendum, it put a powerful new weapon in the hands of the opponents of the Liberal-Radicals. The Catholic-Conservatives were not slow to appreciate the importance of this new 'referendum weapon'.

From now on any new law which savoured in the least of being anti-federal was opposed by referendum by the Catholic-Conservatives. Between 1874 and 1891, when the Peoples' Initiative was brought in, they had recourse to the referendum in order to block legislation no fewer than 19 times. These included opposition to the nationalisation of the railways, the issuing of bank notes and certain proposals on education. Only six times were they unsuccessful; they were so effective that political chaos threatened.

The outcome of it all was that the Liberal-Radicals were compelled to come to an understanding with the Catholic-Conservatives by conceding a seat in the Federal Council to the latter. Politically this proved to be extremely wise because from then on the two parties began to become reconciled and to find that they had common interests, especially so after the Worker Movement came into being and the Social-Democratic Party was founded. As a result of this reconciliation, the Catholic-Conservatives now allowed to become law legislation which previously they had blocked, such as nationalisation of the railways, the unification of the military system and a sickness and accident law. By the outbreak of the First World War the Swiss political climate had so changed that the Catholic-Conservatives and the Liberal-Radicals had become allies in their opposition to the Social-Democrats, whom they regarded as a common political opponent in disputes over social matters.

12

THE WORKER MOVEMENT AND DEVELOPMENT TO POLITICAL PARTNERSHIP

In Switzerland the Worker Movement began in a modest way. Socialist Movements had been founded, mostly by foreigners, in several Swiss towns and in 1873 a worker alliance between trade unions, worker educational societies, and sick benefit societies was founded.

In the 1830's the Grütli Society had also been founded by Democrats who sympathised with the working man and wished to improve his moral and material well-being through education. The Grütli Society acted as a connecting link between the Democratic and Worker Movements.

In 1880 the worker alliance was disbanded and the Schweizerische Gewerkschaftsbund (Swiss Trade Union Alliance), a purely trade union organization based on Socialist principles, was founded. This was followed in 1888 by the founding of a political wing to the Worker Movement at national level, namely the Sozialdemokratische Partei der Schweiz (Swiss Social Democratic Party). This then prompted the founding at national level of the Freisinnig-demokratische Partei der Schweiz (Swiss Liberal-Radical Party) in 1894, and the Catholic Conservatives then established the Christlichdemokratische Volkspartei der Schweiz (Swiss Christian-Democratic Peoples' Party) at national level

53

between 1894 and 1912.

Before the First World War about half the members of the Swiss Trade Union Alliance were foreigners, and as they had no political rights they had to resort to strike action in order to be effective. They became radical in their outlook and the Swiss Trade Union Alliance followed by abandoning its position of political neutrality and adopting a programme of class war. Influenced by the trade unions, the Social-Democratic Party also now drew up a political programme which was affected by Marxism, but in keeping with its democratic tradition its main political demand remained the same, namely the introduction of the proportional representation voting system.

The introduction of the Factory Law of 1877 was an early success for the Worker Movement as it greatly improved working conditions in the factories. A second Factory Law followed in 1914, but it did not come into effect until after the war.

The First World War was accompanied by tremendous dissatisfaction and social unrest in Switzerland. Added to the deep divergence of sympathy for the contending powers in the war - the French speaking Swiss looked for a French victory, while those who were German speaking hoped for success for the Germans - there was additional widespread resentment in the Swiss Romande over the predominent position of the German speaking part of Switzerland. There was also bitter resentment over the disproportionate amount of suffering experienced by the various social classes. Whilst certain sections of the people were making large profits from the war, particularly industrialists and the farmers who benefited from the 130 per cent rise in food prices between 1914 and 1918, others were close to starvation. On being called up an ordinary soldier lost his job automatically. His family received 14 days further pay and then they were left to their own devices. This caused intense hardship to many Swiss families and in the second half of the war the Worker Movement became more radical. The Olten Committee led by Robert Grimm was formed and led the movement in the critical days of 1918/19.

There was a general strike in November 1918, but it collapsed after three days when the Federal Council issued an ultimatum and threatened to call in the troops. The effects of this strike were, however, more enduring.

In reponse to the activities of the Worker Movement the bourgeois political parties now formed an anti-socialist alliance. The farmers withdrew their support from the Freisinnig-demokratische Partei and formed their own party which was later to become the Schweizerische Volkspartei (Swiss Peoples' Party). In 1918, some time before a general election, proportional representation to the National Council was introduced and as a result of this the Liberal-Radicals lost their overall majority in the two chambers which they had held since 1848. The new farmers' party won 14 per cent of the seats in the National Council where they formed an alliance with the Liberal-Radicals and the Christian-Democrats against the Social-Democrats and this offset the gains made by the latter. As a result of this election the Christian-Democrats were given a second seat in the Federal Council.

Political tension ran high during the first half of the 1920's but it gradually quietened down as a result of sensible social legislation and an improvement in economic conditions.

But soon a new world economic crisis set in. It brought with it National Socialism in Germany and in Switzerland many critics of Swiss Democracy which was condemned as being too hesitant and ineffective. There was widespread support, at this time, for the more direct methods of the Fascist leaders.

An initiative was launched for the revision of the Federal Constitution in favour of these more direct methods. The political climate in Switzerland was now tense, but as had happened so often previously in Swiss history, a sense of national unity and patriotism prevailed over the disruptive political forces. The Social-Democrats joined the Liberal-Radicals to oppose the referendum and defeated it.

Since the early 1920's there had been a certain softening of attitudes within the Worker Movement. It had become more pragmatic and co-operative and participated in elections, initiatives and referenda.

The trade unions used this period to negotiate general work agreements, and to establish a position of equality between themselves and the bourgeois economic organizations. The threat of Fascism, and the shameful treatment of trade unionists in Germany were responsible for the eventual abandonment of extreme political attitudes by the Swiss Worker Movement and for its future co-operation with the establishment.

This radical re-orientation on the part of the Swiss trade unions and the Social Democratic Party constituted a change of attitude from a revolutionary posture to a social reform outlook which paved the way for the integration of the two into Swiss bourgeois society and organization. It was to prove of great value during the Second World War, when national unity became of prime importance.

In 1935, the Swiss Social Democratic Party adopted a new programme which acknowledged bourgeois democracy and armed national defence. In 1937, the Metal and Watch-making Industry Trade Union reached a permanent understanding with the employers' association, known as the Peace Agreement, in which direct action in the form of strikes and lock-outs was abjured in favour of negotiated agreement. This peace agreement set an example to other industries and commercial concerns, so much so that it may be regarded as the coming of age of industrial relations in Switzerland, because since that date there has been no major strike.

The change of attitude of the Social-Democrats meant that from now on they could be accepted as partners in democratic government, but full maturity in Swiss political relationships was to have to wait until after the Second World War. It came in 1959, when it was decided to re-constitute the Federal Council according to what is known as the 'magic formula'. According to this agreed formula the Federal Council was henceforth to comprise of two members from each of the following parties, Freisinnig-demokratische Partei der Schweiz (Liberal-Radical), Christlichdemokratische Volkspartei der

Schweiz (Christian-Democrat) and Sozialdemokratische Partei der Schweiz (Social-Democrat) and one member from the Schweizerische Volkspartei (Centre party). By adopting this formula, the Swiss Government became a broadly based coalition government; so broadly based that it could count on the support of more than three-quarters of the members of the Swiss Parliament. Because of this it has been deemed the most stable government in the world.

Just as the Swiss after the Battle of Marignano in 1515, adopted a policy of neutrality and rejected external aggression forever, they had now reached a stage where internal strife could be abandoned also and be replaced by sensible political co-operation and partnership.

13

PARTNERSHIP IN TRADE AND
INDUSTRY

During the first half of the 19th century there were far-reaching economic developments in trade and industry and especially in agriculture.

The Swiss have always had problems with food supply because the country has few natural resources, is remote from the sea, and possesses only a limited amount of productive land. It was these reasons which prompted early industrialisation.

It was during Napoleon's 'Mediation' that Swiss industry began to transfer from handwork in the home to factory production and for the factories to become centred on the banks of rivers and streams in order to take advantage of the cheap water power available to them. As a result of this, between 1800 and 1850 the percentage of workers in agriculture declined by eight per cent and those employed in the service industries increased by two per cent and those in industry by six per cent.

This industrialisation was prompted by Napoleon's economic blockade of England. It was only because there was a plentiful supply of cheap labour in the country areas that the Swiss were able to compete with the more industrialised England, and so become industrialised themselves. Mechanisation, which enabled a transition from handwork in the home to factory production, began in the cotton industry in 1801 when the first Swiss spinning-mill was opened in St Gallen. It was quickly followed by many others, so much so that by 1814 traditional hand-spinning was almost a thing of the past in Switzerland.

This rapid mechanisation of the spinning industry and the development of the clock and watch-making industry in western Switzerland led to the founding of a Swiss machine building industry.

The chemical industry was also stimulated by the requirements of the textile industry. In 1824 the first machine for the manufacture of paper was set up in Switzerland, and in 1819 in Vevey the first chocolate factory had already been opened.

By 1830, per head of the population, Switzerland was exporting more than any other European country. But Swiss industry laboured under great difficulties during this period. Firstly there were internal customs barriers between the cantons which hampered domestic trading, and weights and measures differed from canton to canton, as did currency; although all this would be rectified in the new constitution of 1848. Secondly the country lacked a modern transport system - the first railway on Swiss soil was not opened until 1844.

But an even more profound change occurred in agriculture during this period between 1800 and 1850 due to a variety of reasons. First it was early in the 19th century that a partnership began to develop between the three factors of agricultural production, namely the landowners, the capitalists and the agricultural workers, all of whom had a vested interest in a healthy Swiss agriculture. Secondly, interest in Swiss agriculture was stimulated at this time by far-sighted agriculturalists and farming societies, such as mountain co-operatives. A better breeding of livestock was encouraged, the practice of leaving land fallow for a year abandoned in favour of a rotation of crops and the production of animal foodstuffs. The promotion of stall-feeding led to an accumulation of manure, which again by its application, and that of fertilisers, led to increased productivity; so much so that by 1850 Switzerland was almost self-supporting as regards her requirements of grain.

The continental blockade during the Napoleonic Wars led to the development of the production of sugar-beet and the first sugar refineries were opened in Switzerland in 1810. Other branches of agriculture, such as root crops, fruit and milk production developed correspondingly during this period.

The 'agricultural revolution' was also furthered by the abolition of tithes and feudal dues, by the dividing up and privatisation of the use of common land and by the reclaiming of marshland by drainage; and the correction of watercourses, the most famous of which was the Linth Correction.

14

THE LINTH CORRECTION

If the second exodus of the Helvetii in 58BC, in search of a promised land in Gaul, may be regarded as the first major joint commercial endeavour on the part of the Swiss people, then surely the draining of the lower valley of the River Linth, in the early 19th century must claim to be the second. Such a massive constructional undertaking could not possibly be carried out without the close co-operation of all the cantons, the local communes and private citizens. Previously the cantons had administered their domestic affairs independently, so this was the first big joint cantonal venture in the non-military field.

Originally the lakes of Zurich and Wallen were joined and formed a 50 mile stretch of water. Over the centuries the sand and rubble washed down from the mountains by the River Linth had silted up the lower valley and divided the lake in two. The two lakes, however, were still connected by the River Máág, which was joined by the River Linth near Ziegelbrücke and the two then flowed into Lake Zurich.

During the 18th century it was decided to strip the timber from the Glarnerland mountains, below which the River Linth flowed, in order to supply the domestic textile and building industries and also for heating and exports to Holland. The consequent soil erosion caused masses of earth and rock to slide down into the valley below and dam up Lake Wallen, raising its water-level by five metres. Only a diversion of the course of the River Linth, and a deepening of the connection between the two lakes would solve the problem. The first correction project was presented to the cantons in 1784, but the political will and the necessary finances to put it into effect were, as yet, lacking.

But action would have to be taken, and added to the urgency was a growing Swiss national consciousness and political solidarity which required expression in some joint effort by the cantons, communes, trade and industry and the private citizen. The draining of the lower Linth Valley offered the opportunity for just such an effort.

In 1807 a Zurich town councillor, Johann Konrad Escher, revised the original plans for the correction of the River Linth and constructed a diversionary canal, called the Mollis Canal, which detached the River Linth from the River Máág, so that it now flowed directly into Lake Wallen. At the same time he constructed a deeper canal between the two lakes, reducing Lake Wallen to its original level. The marshland between the two lakes, which hitherto had been malaria infested, could now be drained and cultivated.

Even today such an enterprise would be regarded as ambitious, but for the Swiss of the early 19th century, with the limited and primitive resources which they had at their disposal, it was a colossal undertaking. Fortunately full participation was forthcoming. The project cost more than a million Swiss francs and this sum was subscribed by the cantons, communes and private citizens. The return the investors received on their money, in the form of added value to the land, was such that the venture set a precedent for future joint enterprises, and stimulated future economic planning on a national scale.

15

THE SWISS RAILWAYS

The success of the Linth Correction paved the way for the building of the Swiss railway network.

The first railway on Swiss soil was opened in 1844 and ran from Strasbourg to Basel. The first genuinely Swiss railway was opened three years later from Zurich to Baden. It was intended that the line should run further to Basel, but the Aargau Cantonal Parliament refused to pass a law which would have empowered the expropriation of the necessary land for the building of the railway as far as Basel, and so for the moment the line had to end at Baden.

The situation improved, however, with the introduction of the new Federal Constitution of 1848, for while the railways are not specifically mentioned on it, provision was made for their eventual purchase by the Federal State or for the Federal State, if necessary, to subsidise them. The Federal State could do nothing itself to build railways, because its coffers were empty. On the 1 May 1850 the Federal Assembly passed a law which would henceforth make the expropriation of land for railway construction possible, and thereby they created the legal basis for the construction of the Swiss railways. In the same year Robert Stephenson the son of George Stephenson, together with another foreigner, was commissioned by the Federal Council to work out a plan for a Swiss railway network.

There was tremendous controversy about the routes of the proposed railway lines and also there were political differences as to whether they should be state or privately owned. In July 1852 both the National Council and the States Council opted for a privately-owned railway network, and from that moment railway fever took possession of the Swiss economy. The required capital for the building of the railways was largely provided by newly-founded banks, but the cantons, communes and private citizens also played their part. By 1910 around 3,000 miles of railways had been built in Switzerland, and to these must be added the numerous narrow-gauge railways in the mountains. Since that date the Swiss railway network has remained much the same.

In order not to be outdone by the Austrians who had built the Brenner railway in 1867, and the French who had tunnelled Mont Cenis in 1871, the Swiss decided that they too would build a north-south international railway connection, but they lacked the necessary money. Fortunately both the Italians and the Germans showed interest in a St Gotthard railway line and were prepared to help to finance it. Work was begun on the project in 1872, but it took ten years to complete the St Gotthard tunnel and the venture had to be rescued financially by the Federal State in 1876.

In the last quarter of the century certain other Swiss railways also got into financial difficulties and as a result of this the five biggest companies were nationalised in 1898.

In 1906 the Simplon tunnel came into operation, as did the Jungfrau railway in 1912 which ran up to the highest railway station in the world. In 1913 the Lötschberg line was opened and in 1957 the first high speed Trans-European expresses were introduced to connect Switzerland with neighbouring countries.

The construction of the Swiss railways offers the third, and perhaps the best example of Swiss joint commercial endeavour. The building of the St Gotthard and Jungfrau railways alone required tremendous feats of constructional engineering, and they are still regarded as two of the constructional wonders of the world. The building of the Swiss railways, once more, was only made possible by a realistic partnership over the years between

the Federal State, cantons, communes, industry, the Swiss
banking-system and the people.

16

THE BANKING SYSTEM

It was the building of the railways which prompted the founding of the larger Swiss banks, such as the Schweizerische Kreditanstalt and the Schweizerische Bankverein. It was the electrification of industry and the towns which was responsible for a whole network of local and regional banks. This electrification created a wide demand for capital, and in order to supply that capital banks had to be established. It was during this period that most of the cantonal banks were founded, and even the cantons themselves participated in this development of industry.

The leading Swiss insurance companies were established in order to cover the risks attendant upon this increased industrial activity, and here again the Swiss banks were involved.

By the end of the century the Swiss possessed a highly developed industrial structure and well-established banking and insurance systems. This had been achieved through close co-operation between industry and the banks, plus a certain amount of aid from outside, and also the support of the cantons and people.

During the 20th century the banks and insurance companies continued to expand, until by 1980 there were some 473 banking firms in Switzerland of which 220 were regional or savings banks.

Switzerland has more publicly owned or publicly controlled banks than any other country in the world. These include the Swiss National Bank, which is a special

statutory public limited company, 29 cantonal banks and
40 regional or savings banks. By 1984 these Swiss banking
institutions were employing 98,000 people and the
aggregate of their balance sheet totals (Bilanzsummen)
amounted to more than three times that of the Swiss
Gross National Product (GNP) in that year.

The Swiss insurance companies, too, greatly extended
their activities and in 1985 they earned Sfr 660 million
abroad.

The banks have always enjoyed strong support from
the Swiss, thanks to the confidence that the people have in
the sound financial policies which they pursue and also
because the Swiss are one of the thriftiest people in the
world.

17

PARTNERSHIP AFTER 1848

For a short time after 1848 the doctrine of free trade held sway in Europe, but around 1874 an economic depression set in which brought with it a reappraisal of economic thinking. European countries took fright and began to adopt protectionist measures and Switzerland was no exception to this. The various industries closed their ranks by forming national trade association alliances and in 1870 the Schweizerische Handels- und Industrieverein (Swiss Trade and Industry Association) was founded. This was followed by the Schweizerische Gewerbeverein (Swiss Trade Association) and farmers and workers national organizations followed. All received subsidies from the Federal State, because the Federal administration was not in a position to offer the necessary supervision of economic affairs, and so had to rely on these national bodies. This led to a close co-operation between the Federal State administration and trade and industry, a partnership which by the outbreak of the First World War had developed determined, influential, extra-parliamentary procedures.

During the latter half of the 19th century certain Swiss industries began to develop their overseas markets and so lay the foundation of a Swiss commercial empire overseas. To further this objective, Swiss trading companies began to be founded abroad. While some of these trading companies had considerable birth pangs, many managed to survive and consolidate themselves in overseas trade.

The prosperous First World War Years were followed

by a period of depression in which exports sank to a third of their former value and some banks went bankrupt. The machine industry benefited at this time by the decision to electrify the railways, and the Swiss chemical industry kept its head above water by forming cartels with French and German firms. Until 1934 the Swiss economy was able to maintain itself, thanks to a thriving building industry which was able to absorb many unemployed workers from the exporting industries, but eventually the building industry also became depressed with the result that in 1936 there were 124,000 out of work in Switzerland. Between the two world wars there was little economic growth and during the Second World War it was merely a question of survival.

After the Second World War Switzerland was fortunate in having the necessary requirements for a dramatic economic leap forward. Her factories had emerged unscathed and she had the necessary labour force and capital at her disposal. She poured money into industrial research, new technology and the education of her work force with the result that in 20 years, between 1964 and 1984, her Gross National Product (GNP) increased by over 50 per cent.

Apart from the recession of the seventies, the post war years have been a boom-time for Switzerland, during which certain industrial firms in the machine and engineering, chemical and food-processing industries have attained world rank. It has been a period of full employment; the unemployment rate in July 1986 was only 0.7 per cent, and more than three-quarters of a million foreign workers are employed in the country. Switzerland has a low rate of inflation and one of the highest standards of living in the world.

Much of Switzerland's success can be attributed to sensible co-operation and partnership between the various agents to her economic activity. Sensible co-operation between the Federal State, cantons, communes, trade and industry and the Swiss banking system in such projects as the draining of the lower River Linth valley and the construction of the Swiss railways which were prerequisites of Swiss economic development later. Sensible co-operation between the Federal administration and the national umbrella organizations representing Swiss trade and industry and the trade unions, which have been mentioned previously, laid the foundations of future Swiss prosperity.

18

PARTNERSHIP IN ADMINISTRATION

Since the forming of the Swiss Federal State in 1848, partnership has also been much in evidence in the administration of Swiss affairs. In order to understand how this partnership is effected, it is necessary to know something of how Switzerland is constituted.

The Swiss Confederation is made up of 26 independent states called cantons (six of which rank as half cantons), and these are divided up into about 3,060 local authorities called communes. In 1848, these cantons, which had been independent states for many years, came together to form the Swiss Federal State, and in creating this higher authority they strengthened their relationship to each other without, at the same time, forfeiting their individual independence too greatly.

Partnership between the Federal State, cantons and communes is effected in Switzerland by means of federalism. One definition of a federal state is a 'union of government in which several states while independent in home affairs, combine for national and general purposes'. Such roughly is Switzerland, namely a federation of sovereign states which, while enjoying a large amount of independence, are prepared to sacrifice a certain amount of their autonomy to a higher authority, namely the Federal State, in respect of national matters and those of common interest.

At the founding of the Swiss National State it was decided that at national level political power should be divided between three political agencies, namely the

Legislature (Parliament), the Executive (Federal Council) and the Judiciary (Federal Supreme Court). In order to spread political authority even more widely, it was decided that Parliament should consist of two chambers, to be elected by the people democratically. There would be the National Council to represent the people, and the States Council to represent the cantons. Together these two chambers would form the Federal Assembly. The executive was to be the Federal Council, which may be termed the Government or Cabinet and this body was to comprise seven councillors, to be elected by the Federal Assembly and its job would be to rule the country.

The Federal Council is run as a college. Each federal councillor is head of one of seven departments, namely foreign affairs, home affairs, justice and police, military, finance, economic affairs, transport and energy. The Federal Council takes all decisions jointly and responsibilty is shared. Consequently there is no such thing as a vote of no confidence in respect of Swiss Federal councillors. This form of political partnership makes for great stability.

In Switzerland there is also no such thing as an official head of state. The nearest approach to one is the President of the Federal Council, but he is only allowed to be president for one year and has no real authority. Throughout his year of office he remains head of a department and at the end of his year of office he reverts back to being one of the seven and a fellow cabinet minister takes his place as president.

At cantonal level political partnership is reflected in much the same way in the cantonal political institutions. As the cantons are free, in certain areas, to enact their own laws, each has a legislative body. In five of the cantons, namely Appenzell Ausserrhoden, Appenzell Innerrhoden, Obwalden, Nidwalden and Glarus, this legislative body is known as the Landsgemeinde, a public assembly which meets in the open air annually, transacts the main cantonal business and elects cantonal officials. The other cantons have cantonal parliaments, housed in parliament buildings and their legislative bodies are usually called Kantonsrat (Cantonal Council), Grosser Rat

(Great Council) or Landrat (Cantonal Council). The cantons also have executive bodies, or governments usually called Regierungsrat (Government Council), Kleiner Rat (Small Council) or Staatsrat (Cantonal Council), which are elected by the people.

The communes, although subject to cantonal law and authority, nevertheless enjoy a certain amount of autonomy. Each has a commune assembly (Gemeindeversammlung), which all enfranchised commune members are free to attend, or in larger communes a Grosser Gemeinderat (Great Commune Council) or Grosser Stadtrat (Great Town Council), all of which are elected by the people. The people also elect a smaller executive body usually known as the Engere Gemeinderat (Small Commune Council) or the Kleine Stadtrat (Small Town Council), to execute the decisions of the larger assembly. The president of these executive bodies is called either Gemeindepräsident, Gemeindemann or Stadtpräsident. The running of commune affairs is effected by various committees responsible to the higher commune bodies. All important decisions taken by a commune political authority may be subjected to a peoples' referendum and in many communes expenditure over a certain amount may also be subject to a veto by the enfranchised citizens.

At cantonal level the citizen's political rights are perhaps more extensive than at national level, because in addition to the right to vote, hold office, the referendum and the peoples' initiative, the enfranchised citizens also have the right to elect the members of the cantonal governments. In many cantons, in addition to the constitutional initiative there is also the legal initiative, which gives citizens the right to change the law as well as the constitution. In some cases the facultative referendum is extended to include decisions on expenditure over a certain amount.

Co-operation between the cantonal administrative departments and between the Federal and cantonal administration is not only effected by direct contact, but also through various departmental conferences which meet at regular intervals to discuss common problems.

The most important of these are the Directors'
Conferences, where the cantonal directors of a certain
department meet together, with the Federal Department
chief in attendance.

19

TASK SHARING

THE FEDERAL STATE

Just as political authority in Switzerland is shared at Federal, cantonal and commune level by various political powers, so national political tasks and commitments are divided up between the Federal State, the cantons and the communes and are carried out by these either individually or in partnership.

The principal commitments of the Federal State, as laid down in the Federal Constitution are as follows:

To preserve the integrity of the Swiss National State from outside attack,

maintain law and order within and arbitrate in cantonal disputes,

protect the rights and liberties of Swiss citizens and those of trade and industry,

promote the common good by sound economic planning,

co-operate with the cantons in matters of taxation,

guarantee cantonal territories and constitutions,

decide upon peace and war,

negotiate foreign treaties and be responsible for foreign affairs,

be responsible for the army, its weaponry and instruction,

be responsible for civil defence,

maintain an adequate supply of bread and grain for defence purposes,

maintain a healthy farming community and agricultural industry,

erect public works and be responsible for waterworks,
promote utilisation of water supply,
be responsible for forestry,
be responsible for certain police departments and certain
police affairs,
promote scientific research and culture (museums,
Federal Institutions),
build or support higher educational establishments,
ensure the freedom and promote trade and industry
(support threatened branches),
support any economically threatened areas of the
country,
supervise the Swiss National Bank and the banking
system,
supervise the roads and bridges and construct motorways,
supervise rents and prices and protect the customer,
supervise education and promote vocational training,
promote social housing, social security and social
insurance,
supervise health and veterinary affairs,
combat unemployment,
set basic principles for footpath network,
be responsible for the minting of coins and printing of
banknotes,
determine weights and measures and supervise patents,
be responsible for the manufacture and sale of
gunpowder,
determine civic rights, asylum and control of foreigners,
promote sport and gymnastics for youth,
support an indigenous film industry and supervise civil
aviation,
control the distilling of spirits and alcohol,
supervise Federal State finances and promote sound
financial policies,
supervise the Federal administration and appoint certain
public officials,
be responsible for customs dues,
ensure that both Federal and cantonal legislation is
constitutional,
govern the country through the Federal Council,
administer justice through the Judiciary,
legislate by means of the Federal Parliament.

In addition to the above areas, the Federal Constitution of 1874 also authorises the Federal State to legislate in the following fields:

Rail, water and air transport, traffic co-ordination, electric and atomic energy, pipelines (oil and natural gas), fishing, hunting, birdlife and animal protection, environmental protection, foodstuffs and infectious diseases, drugs, poisons, medicines, radio, television and other forms of communication of information, the Penal Code, Civil Code, law of Obligation, bankruptcy law, factory law, social legislation, motoring, cycling and traffic legislation and legislation in respect of certain state- owned firms.

The Federal State also runs the Post Office, telegraphs, telephones (PTT), the state-owned railways (SBB), military workshops, aircraft and explosive factories, the Institutes of Technology of Zurich and Lausanne, the Theological Faculty in Lucerne, the Institute of Pedagogics in St Gallen and the Federal Gymnastics and Sports School in Magglingen. The Federal State also has interests in the watch-making, embroidery and hotel industries and it gives support, when necessary, to the sugar refineries in Aarberg and Frauenfeld. It also gives export guarantees to trade and industry in order to further foreign trade.

The Federal Constitution of 1874 also stipulates what taxes the Federal State may levy, their apportioning between Federal State and cantons and provides a system of fiscal equalisation between the cantons for the subsidies which the Federal State pays to them. The Federal Constitution of 1874 also earmarks certain of the revenue from these taxes for certain specific purposes such as the construction and maintenance of the motorways and social insurance.

The cantons also participate in legislation in certain fields, among these are the control of alcohol, agriculture, area planning, trade, industry and commerce, the utilisation of water power, taxation, roads and bridges, hunting and fishing, schools, sickness and accident insurance, control of foreigners and infectious diseases, among others. The cantons are also responsible for legislation in respect of church affairs, commune affairs and the police, where they are not the responsibility of the Federal State, and in any other field not designated to the Federal State.

THE CANTONS

Certain tasks are the responsibilty of the cantons, either in their own right, or have been deputed to them by the Federal State. To these belong:
The maintenance of law and order in the canton,
supervision of commune affairs,
organization and administration of justice,
certain military obligations (inspections, equipping of troops, arsenals),
the determining of a cantonal budget,
running of intermediate schools and eight cantonal universities,
the administration of church affairs,
protection of water supplies,
promotion of arts and science,
building and maintenance of transit roads,
supervision of savings-banks and sick benefit funds,
administration of cantonal finances and property,
taxation,
the police (where this is not the responsibility of the Federal State),
supervising weights and measures,
the putting into effect of law legislated by the Federal State,
health services (hospitals and institutions)
motor and bicycle licensing,
provision of primary schools,
supervision of hunting and fishing,
control of hotel industry.

In order to carry out these tasks cantonal governments are divided up into departments and these usually include:
Commune affairs,
education,
economic affairs,
social welfare (hospitals and institutions),
public works (electricity, gas, highways, correction of rivers),

police,
military affairs,
religious affairs,
finance and taxation,
justice (courts and prisons),
building,
health,
agriculture/forests,

Concordats are often entered into between cantons in various specialist fields: this is especially true of education and finance.

THE COMMUNES

Certain tasks have either been allocated or belong as of right to the communes. To these may belong the following:

The preservation of public order within the commune,
street-cleaning,
refuse-collection,
fire services,
traffic police,
public transport,
facilitation of the flow of traffic within the commune,
construction of gas, water and electricity works,
maintenance of primary schools,
maintenance of a register of residents,
maintenance of a register of births, marriages and deaths,
maintenence of the poor and orphans,
the management of guardianship,
the adminstration of bankruptcy and debt procedures,
maintenance of a land register,
appointment of a magistrate,
taxation,
burial of the dead,
approval of commune accounts for the past year,
approval of a budget for the coming year,
authorisation of major budget expenditure,
determination of the tax base for the commune tax,
appointment of commune officials,
administration of commune lands and investments,
administration of commune sick-benefit funds,
adminstration of prosecutions,

theatres, libraries, baths and recreation grounds,
civil defence,
arranging of Federal and cantonal elections.

An effective administrative link between the communes
and their cantonal authorities is often furnished by a
Regierungsstatthalter (Governor) who is a full time
cantonal official and operates at district level.

The tasks listed which are carried out by the Federal
State, the cantons and the communes are, of course, by no
means exclusive. A fairly comprehensive list has,
however, been given in order to show the complexity of
administrative organization in Switzerland. From the
above enumeration of the various administrative tasks it is
clear that wherever they are jointly carried out their
execution would be impossible without close co-operation
between the three. Co-operation between the Federal
State and the cantons is largely effected administratively
by Federal and cantonal civil servants and by their
respective departments. The Federal Government and
cantonal government administration is departmentalised
in much the same way, so that the departments of the
Federal Government largely have their equivalent at
cantonal level. This relationship also holds good between
the cantons and communes.

To an outsider this division of political tasks between
the Federal State, the cantons and the communes is
extremely confusing, as it is sometimes for the Swiss
themselves. The determining as to which authority is
responsible for which task can even cause differences of
opinion and long delay. It may be, however, that this is
the price that has to be paid if a maximum of the people
are to be closely involved in the political organization and
running of the country, and if autocratic rule is to be
avoided.

Nevertheless, serious attempts are being made by the
Swiss political authorities to clarify and rationalise the
division of Swiss political commitments between the
Federal State, the cantons and the communes, because
they realise that unless this is done, administrative chaos
could eventually ensue.

20

TAXATION

The political tasks performed by the Federal State, the cantons and the communes have, of course, to be financed and this entails the provision of the required funds. This is effected primarily by taxation, and here again close co-operation is necessary between the Federal State, the cantons and the communes, because all three authorities levy taxes.

When the Federal State was formed in 1848 the cantons renounced their right to collect customs dues and these became the perquisite of the Federal State. In 1874 the Federal State also introduced a tax on military service exemption and in 1888 one on the distilling of spirits. The revenue from these sources was sufficient to finance the Federal State until the outbreak of the First World War, but during that war national expenditure increased so much that the Federal State found it necessary to introduce stamp duties and also direct taxes in order to increase its revenue. This direct taxation eventually developed into the National Defence Tax of 1940 which today is called the Direct Federal Tax. The assessment and collection of the Direct Federal Tax are the responsibility of the 26 cantonal administrations, but the Federal Tax Administration has the right of supervision.

Meanwhile a tax on motor fuel had been introduced in 1929, one on tobacco in 1933 and one on beer in 1934. During the Second World War, in 1941, a turnover tax was introduced and in 1944 an anticipatory with-holding tax, later recoverable by the tax payer. Since 1985

81

motorway charges and a heavy lorry levy have also been in force which have added to Federal funds.

All the taxes which the Federal State is permitted to levy are laid down in the Federal Constitution. The cantons are free to levy any tax other than those for which the Federal State has exclusive authority. Commune taxation is subject to cantonal jurisdiction.

The principal taxes levied by the Federal State are:
Income tax, and net profit and capital tax which constitute the Direct Federal Tax,
anticipatory withholding tax,
stamp duties,
military service exemption tax,
turnover tax,
tobacco tax,
beer tax,
tax on distilling of spirits,
customs dues, (Import and export duties and supplementary excise levies)
motor fuel tax, motorway charges and a heavy goods vehicle levy.

Part of the yield from certain of these taxes goes to the cantons. A large part of the revenue from the motor fuel tax is devoted to the building of the Swiss motorways and the revenue from the taxes from distilling and tobacco go into the Old Age, Bereavement and Disablement Insurance equalisation fund. The anticipatory withholding tax is recoverable by the tax payer providing he or she declares it on their tax declaration form.

The principle cantonal taxes are:
Income and net wealth tax,
poll or household tax,
net profit and capital taxes,
inheritance and gift taxes,
capital gains tax,
transfer of property tax,
real estate tax,
motor vehicle and bicycle tax,
tax on dogs,
entertainment tax,
lottery winnings tax,

stamp duties,
tax on hydraulic power-stations,
visitors tax and
sundry other taxes.

Certain of these taxes are levied by all cantons, but others are only imposed by some of the cantons and these varyingly.

The principal commune taxes are:
Income and net-wealth taxes,
poll or household tax,
net profit and capital taxes,
inheritance and gift taxes,
real estate tax,
transfer of property tax,
capital gains tax,
tax on dogs,
entertainment tax,
lottery winnings tax,
trade tax,
visitors tax and
sundry other taxes.

Here again certain taxes are common to all communes, but others vary from commune to commune.

In many cases commune taxes are combined with cantonal taxes and in others they are supplementary to them. Church taxes are often administered in the same way. The cantons may empower both districts and church parishes to levy taxes.

The Swiss tax system reflects the federal nature of Switzerland. All the Swiss cantons have their tax law and the communes may levy taxes independently or within the framework of basic cantonal tax rates, but always only as authorised by cantonal tax law. Certain of the yield from cantonal taxes goes to the Federal State. The people themselves determine what type of tax shall be levied at both Federal and cantonal level and in many cases they have a say in the fixing of the tax base and rates. The top level of the direct Federal taxes is laid down in the Federal Constitution and can only be altered with the consent of the people and cantons.

The extent of the co-operation which exists between

the various Swiss tax authorities may be seen from the fact that the Direct Federal Tax is collected by the cantonal tax authorities in all cantons except St Gallen where it is collected by the commune tax departments. Cantonal and commune taxes are collected varyingly by the cantonal and commune tax authorities, either individually or both together by the cantonal authorities.

There is one great disadvantage in Switzerland not having a uniform tax system, namely that there are differences in the tax burden which the various cantons and communes have to bear. These vary not only from canton to canton but also between communes in the same canton. This is especially true of income and wealth taxes, but less marked in respect of the taxes on consumption, because these are mostly levied by the Federal State. This disadvantage, however, is the price that has to be paid for the large amount of freedom which the various Swiss political bodies enjoy in respect of financial matters. A uniform tax system could only be put into effect if the cantons and communes were to be deprived of their autonomy in the tax field and the Federal State alone were permitted to levy taxes. This, however, would lead to a reduction in cantonal power and an increase in the power of the Federal State would ensue which is something the Swiss are anxious to avoid. Moreover, it is questionable if a completely centralised Switzerland could survive for long, because basically the country is constituted federally.

In order to reduce the difference in tax burdens, which the cantons and communes have to carry in Switzerland, the Federal political authorities have set up inter-cantonal and inter-communal compensation funds. The cantons are divided into three groups according to their financial strength, weak, average and strong and the monies which the Federal State transfers to the cantons is apportioned accordingly. This equalisation enables the poorer cantons to reduce their taxes. The same principle also holds good in the apportioning of monies from the cantons to the communes. From this description of the Swiss tax system may be seen the amount of partnership and solidarity displayed towards each other by the various political entities.

21

SOCIAL SECURITY

Perhaps the best example of co-operation in Switzerland between the Federal State, the cantons, trade and industry and the people is in the provision of social welfare.

The Swiss social welfare structure is largely supported by three pillars. The first pillar provides for a basic existence in retirement, or should misfortune strike a person, and comprises insurance against old age, bereavement (being widowed or orphaned) and invalidity. In addition it provides compensation for loss of earnings as a result of being called up into the Army or Civil Defence. The first pillar is jointly financed by a percentage deduction from wages or salaries to which is added an equal amount from the employer, by subsidies from the Federal State and cantons, and finally by interest on Federal investments which have been put away over a long period of time specifically for this purpose. The first pillar comprises old age and bereavement (widows and orphans) insurance, known as AHV, disablement insurance (IV), and earnings indemnity (EO).

The second pillar is occupational provision for old age, disablement and bereavement (widows and orphans) which is known as BVG. This is financed solely by a percentage deduction from wages or salaries to which is added a similar amount from the employer. This second pillar (BVG) is meant to supplement AHV, so that the standard of living to which a person has been accustomed may be maintained. The third pillar is the provision made by the individual through private insurance to supplement his or her needs should misfortune befall them or in old age.

In this provision for Swiss people against the vagaries of life, the employee, employer, Federal State, cantons and private individuals all co-operate to provide the necessary insurance, and in that it is the duty of the communes to provide a safety net for those who cannot insure, they too participate in the provision of social welfare in Switzerland.

Insurance against accidents is compulsory for all employees. Since 1919 the Swiss National Insurance Institute (SUVA) in Lucerne, a private organization, has run this department of social security. Other forms of social security in Switzerland include Unemployment Insurance (AV) and in certain instances health insurance, though this is not universally compulsory. These other forms of social insurance are also financed by a deduction from wages or salaries to which is added a similar amount from the employer. In exceptional circumstances the Federal State and the cantons may also contribute to unemployment insurance. All this social insurance in Switzerland is adminstered by numerous Federal, cantonal and private insurance funds, known as Ausgleichskassen or Krankenkassen.

22

THE HEALTH SERVICES

The provision of health care is a shared commitment between the Federal State, the cantons and the communes. In the field of public health only a limited number of tasks lie within the authority of the Federal State, among them the combating of infectious diseases, the control of foodstuffs, protection from radiation, the control of poisons and drugs, medicinal testing and social insurance. In these fields the Federal State legislates and the cantons execute that legislation.

Basically it is the cantons themselves which are responsible for the health services in Switzerland. To these responsibilities belong the provision of medical care, preventive medicine and the passing of police regulations in health matters, providing these do not fall within the jurisdiction of the Federal State. The cantons have wide discretionary powers in the provision of health services. Some, for example, run their own hospitals, while others subsidise private hospitals.

It is the cantons which legislate in such matters as school medical and dental services or the provision of old people's homes and social welfare institutions. Here the execution of these regulations may be deputed to a lower level, namely to that of the communes. The communes are especially responsible for the provision of social welfare, care of the elderly and home medical and social services. The communes also have tasks delegated to them by the Federal State, such as the provision of first aid posts in air raid shelters and the provision of institutions for the handicapped, for which tasks they receive subsidies from the Federal State.

The fourth partner in the Swiss health field is the private sector. Many important functions of the Swiss health services are performed by private organizations which operate private hospitals, institutions for the handicapped and sick-benefit and accident insurance funds. These private organizations may be commissioned by the Federal State, the cantons or the communes to whose respective supervision they are subject. In Switzerland in 1985, there were some 16,473 doctors in practice and around 913 hospitals nationwide.

23

EDUCATION

The Federal Constitution lays down, 'that the cantons shall provide adequate primary school instruction', and that it shall be under Federal supervision, free and accessible to children of all confessions, without prejudice to freedom of belief or conscience.

Once again the federal principle is in evidence, in that the communes are usually allowed to run their own primary schools, but only within the limits laid down in cantonal law. Instruction in the primary schools is supervised by the Federal authorities. The Federal State may intervene if the cantonal educational authorities fail to carry out their obligations.

The duration of the compulsory school period varies between eight and nine years according to the canton and incorporates primary, intermediate and upper school education.

The intermediate and upper schools usually come under the jurisdiction and administration of the cantons, and as a result of this there are many different school systems in Switzerland. It might be expected that as a result of this chaos would ensue, but this is not the case because all these school systems must conform to Federal State educational requirements and consequently they do not digress far from each other. Co-ordination between the cantons in educational affairs is also furthered by a concordat for school co-ordination which was signed by most cantons in 1970, and also by the Federal Conference of Directors of Cantonal Education (EDK) and its various committees, and by four regional conferences for education in Switzerland, of which all the cantons are members.

The Federal State educational authorities exercise influence over the cantons in that they are allowed to stipulate minimum standards for certain final upper school examinations, and thereby they are able to exert influence indirectly over the curriculum in these subjects.

The Federal State exerts a more direct influence on vocational education and training, for although the running of these vocational educational establishments is also a commitment of the cantons, the Federal State exercises a close supervision through the Federal Department of Trade and Industry (BIGA). These vocational and specialist schools give the theoretical knowledge required of an apprenticeship, and as an apprenticeship is available to every Swiss child, and consequently widespread, these establishments play an important role in Swiss educational life.

Of the ten Swiss universities (Hochschulen) eight are run by the cantons and two by the Federal State. There is a university of Pedagogics at St Gallen and a theological faculty in Lucerne. The Federal State subsidises the cantonal universities heavily, not only as regards ordinary running expenses, but also in respect of research. The work of the Swiss universities is co-ordinated by the University Council (Der Hochschulrat) which is made up of delegates from the cantons with universities, and the Swiss Academic Council (Der Schweizerische Wissenschaftsrat). The Swiss Academic Council also acts as advisor to the Federal Council in university matters.

In 1952 the Swiss National Fund for the Promotion of Scientific Research (Der Schweizerische Nationalfonds zur Förderung der Wissenschaftlichen Forschung) was founded. It is a private organisation but financed by the Federal State. Great stress is placed on research, for only by spending a vast amount of money on research is it possible for a small country like Switzerland to keep ahead, or even abreast, of her industrial competitors.

Here again, in the provision for research joint effort, once more, comes into play. Around 70 per cent of the cost of research is borne by private industry and the rest largely by the Federal State, either by financing its own establishments, by subsidies to private firms, or in grants to the research departments of the universities and other institutions. Switzerland spends around two per cent of her Gross Domestic Product (GDP) on research.

24

LEGISLATION

The Federal Council, the Houses of Parliament, the cantons and the people are all partners to the legislative process.

Participation can be seen to begin in the election of members to the Houses of Parliament. The National Council, which is representative of the people, comprises 200 members divided proportionately between the cantons, and is elected by the proportional representation voting system. The States Council, which represents the cantons, has 46 members (two members for each full canton and one for each half canton), but is elected mainly by the majority voting system. These two houses meeting together form the Federal Assembly and this body elects the seven Federal councillors who form the Federal Council or Government.

There is also partnership in the initiation of Swiss legislation, because proposed legislation may stem from the Federal Council itself, from members of Parliament in the form of a motion or postulate to the Federal Council for its consideration, from a canton by means of a cantonal initiative, or by a people's initative with signatures from 100,000 enfranchised citizens, collected within 18 months.

If the Federal Council accepts any of these three initiatives, or decides to promote its own proposed legislation, it will draft an outline measure which it will send to the cantons for their consideration and also submit the proposed measure to a general hearing

(Vernehmlassung) at which any interested parties may offer their comment or criticism. The Federal Council can then amend the proposed Bill accordingly and submit it to the two Houses of Parliament for debate.

To become law the Bill must be accepted by both Houses of Parliament which, as we have seen, are representative of the people and cantons.

But the participation of the people and cantons does not stop here, because if the two Houses of Parliament do approve the Bill and it is ratified by the Government, it still needs the direct or tacit approval of the cantons and people before it can become law.

If the Bill would in any way permanently change the Federal Constitution then it must be subjected to an obligatory referendum of the people and cantons. If it does not permanently change the Federal Constitution, it is likely to come within the domain of the facultative or optional referendum whereby 50,000 enfranchised voters or eight cantons may demand a referendum on the Bill within 90 days. From this it may be seen that not only do the people and cantons participate in the process of Federal legislation in Switzerland, but that they also have the last word. The same is also true of cantonal legislation.

25

THE JUDICIARY

As we have already seen, the right to legislate in Switzerland is the preserve of the Federal State and the cantons. Legislation in certain fields is the exclusive right of the Federal State, in others it is that of the cantons and yet in others it belongs to both. The commune assemblies are not allowed to enact actual laws; they may only pass regulations. The cantons may enact any laws other than those which come within the province of the Federal State. Federal law, cantonal law and regulations introduced by the communes are all subject to the obligatory or facultative referendum.

All the legislation passed by the Federal State and the cantons is put into effect by the cantonal authorities. The communes have no courts. Although there are certain district courts, these are only really arbitration courts. The first really effective courts are the cantonal courts and these usually comprise a high court, an assize court, a court of appeal, a commercial court and an administrative court. Above all these courts is the Federal Supreme Court in Lausanne.

The policing of the country is basically the task of the cantons, but here again federalism is in evidence because certain police duties have been delegated to the communes, and the Federal State is directly responsible for the police foreign department. There are also police courts in Switzerland for minor offences.

An interesting feature in the administration of justice in Switzerland is that people convicted of less serious offences, namely whose sentence is 18 months or less in detention, prison or institute of correction, may have their sentence deferred for a period of probation. If the offender is called upon to serve the sentence, it may be in the form of part-time imprisonment, such as weekends or partial imprisonment where the convicted person continues to do his or her job and serve the sentence in their free time.

There is also the Federal Insurance Court, which is an independent social security court within the Federal Supreme Court. It deals with disputes in respect of social and military insurance. There are also military courts in Switzerland which adjudicate on violations of the military penal code.

The cantons are responsible for the execution of sentences passed by the Federal and cantonal courts.

26

SOLIDARITY TOWARDS AGRICULTURE

An especial example of solidarity in Switzerland is that displayed by the non-agricultural community towards their fellows who work on the land, particularly those who work in the remote mountainous areas.

This enlightened attitude is partly due to Switzerland's unique agricultural situation. It is a mountainous country with only a quarter of its land truly fertile and in consequence has always had great difficulty in feeding its population. With the result that agriculture has always occupied a position of importance, not only in the economy, but also in the minds of the Swiss people. Many families still have close connections with the land and consequently still retain a special affection for it, which makes them sympathetic towards the farming community and therefore prepared to make sacrifices for it.

The Federal authorities must also adopt sympathetic attitudes towards Swiss agriculture, because in accordance with the Federal Constitution the Federal State has an obligation to support and protect any branch of the economy which is threatened or in difficulty, and Swiss agriculture falls into this category.

A 100 years ago more than half of the Swiss population were engaged in agriculture, today it is about 6 per cent, such has been the migration from the countryside to the towns. In order to stem any further reduction in the agricultural labour force, especially in the mountainous areas, an Agricultural Act was passed in 1951 which guarantees to the skilled farm worker a comparable wage with workers in other occupations. In 1952 it was decided to introduce household allowances for agricultural workers and a child allowance for agricultural workers and small farmers. These grants are financed by premiums paid by the farmer, plus subsidies from public funds. All these subsidies and allowances to the farming community must eventually be met by the consumer, either in the form of higher prices for agricultural products, or by taxation. In that he or she would appear to meet these largely ungrudgingly, the consumer thereby displays his or her solidarity with the farming community.

The Federal authorities also offer further incentives to Swiss farmers by guaranteeing prices for certain of their products, by granting subsidies and investment grants and by levying customs dues and imposing restrictions on certain imported agricultural products. These again place an added financial burden on the Swiss citizen which he or she would appear to pay quite readily.

27

THE MILITARY SYSTEM

Perhaps the greatest sacrifice made by any one section of the Swiss people towards the good of the community as a whole, is that made by the male population towards the defence of their country. Military service is compulsory for all Swiss males, providing they are not medically unfit or out of the country on legitimate business, in which case they must pay additional tax. As yet there is no alternative civilian service for objectors on grounds of conscience in Switzerland. This is perhaps because the Swiss Army is purely one of defence, and also because there is no professional standing army in Switzerland as the term would be understood in other countries. The Swiss Army is mostly a militia or part time army receiving nominal pay. Certain high ranking officers in the Swiss Army are professional soldiers and there is a hardcore of professional instruction officers, non-commissioned officers for training, a minimum number of personnel for the storage and maintenance of equipment and materials and for administrative purposes who are full time soldiers - the rest are part time soldiers receiving only token pay.

A Swiss man does an initial training of 17 weeks at the age of 20 as a militia-recruit, and a three-week refresher course for the next eight years. Thereafter he does periodical refresher- courses until the age of 50 (55 for officers). If a recruit wishes to become an officer he must do an additional initial training in order to attain the rank of corporal. If he is then adjudged to have the necessary qualities of leadership he may be accepted to train as an officer. If he is accepted, as he rises in rank, he will be expected to do a great deal of administrative work voluntarily.

The militia system does not only apply to the Swiss Army - it has spilled over into civilian life as will be seen later.

28

PARTNERSHIP OF THE PEOPLE

There is also partnership between the generations in Switzerland. This was brought home to me forcibly some time ago when old age pensions were increased. On the morning following the announcement of the increase there were two letters in the Zurich morning paper from elderly pensioners thanking the younger generation for accepting the burden of providing them with the additional pension and apologizing for their not being able to earn it themselves.

On the other hand, responsibilty towards the younger generation was shown by the older generation when the AHV or Old Age and Bereavement Insurance to provide pensions for the retired and widows and orphans was originally conceived. As early as 1925 it was decided that provision should be made in the Federal Constitution for the introduction of such a scheme, and also that, in typical Swiss fashion, it should be jointly financed by the Federal State, the cantons, the employers and the employees. The question arose as to how the Federal State should provide part of its share. Either it could borrow the money, which would have to be paid back later, or the scheme could be deferred until such time as the required funds had been saved and invested so as to yield sufficient interest to make good the contributions required of the Federal State. The Swiss people decided on the more responsible course of deferring the introduction of the scheme until such time as the necessary funds had been saved and invested. In order to do this the Federal tax on tobacco was specifically earmarked for the purpose of financing the scheme and placed in a special fund. This fund grew so rapidly that in 1947 the interest from the investments was deemed sufficient to complete the contribution required of the Federal State and the scheme was introduced. By adopting this policy of saving first, no financial burden was placed on the next generation.

The fact that the older generation has the interests of the younger generation at heart is also demonstrated in the way in which it has controlled the number of foreigners coming into the country so that the jobs of the younger generation would not be jeopardised. Secondly, the older generation has introduced and initially financed a vast scheme of vocational training for youth, whereby every Swiss child on leaving school is offered an apprenticeship. As a result of this there is little teenage unemployment in Switzerland. In this vocational training scheme solidarity between the generations has been further enhanced by the fact that the employers have shown themselves willing to train and qualify in order personally to be responsible for the training of youth in their businesses. Here again it is personal commitment and involvement which makes the partnership work.

29

LENK IN SIMMENTAL

Political and social partnership is perhaps most clearly evident at local level, that is in the commune, because it is here that the individual participates in community affairs the most readily. In order to illustrate how partnership is effected at local level, I have chosen Lenk as an example of a typical average-sized rural Swiss commune.

Lenk is an attractive Alpine village, surrounded on three sides by mountains, some of which rise to 10,000 feet and are covered with snow all the year round. It is a winter-sport and summer resort and also a spa. The hot sulphur spring which bubbles up out of the Bettelberg mountain on the west of the village, and runs into the baths of the spa buildings, is claimed to be the strongest in the Alps and effective against rheumatism and arthritis. In addition to tourism the other main occupation of the people of Lenk is agriculture.

At its southern end the Simmen Valley is connected to the Rhone Valley by the Rawil Pass, but because the original mule track across this pass was never developed into a road, the Rawil Pass has declined in importance as the years have gone by.

Lenk is an average-sized Swiss commune which levies its own taxes, and elects its own political authorities in accordance with Bern cantonal law. The supreme political authority is the Commune Assembly, whose principal duties are to take the most important administrative decisions, certify the commune accounts for the past year, agree on a budget for the coming year, determine the

102

commune tax rate and appoint the various officials required to administer commune affairs.

The Commune Assembly is also responsible for the election of the commune governing body, the Commune Council. The Commune Council consists of a president, vice-president and nine councillors who are chairmen of the several departmental committees which run commune affairs. To these committees belong building, fire-services, finance, welfare, tax, planning primary school, secondary school and domestic science, civil defence and auditing. The work of all these chairmen and their committees is done on a voluntary or semi-voluntary basis. Their work is co-ordinated in the Commune Offices by certain full time officials including the clerk to the commune, treasurer, building inspector, registrar for births, marriages and deaths and their respective secretaries, together with a woman who is responsible for commune welfare finances and payments.

If any member of the commune is elected to office by the Commune Assembly, he or she is compelled to fill that office for three years, unless there is some valid reason for not doing so.

In addition to the political and military service which the menfolk of the Lenk community render to their fellows there are certain other community tasks which they fulfil. They are liable for Civil defence service until they are 60 and also for fire service in the commune. It is possible to seek exemption from fire service, but if a person is exempted he must pay additional tax.

But this by no means exhausts the sacrifice in time and effort which a Swiss male living in Lenk makes on behalf of his fellows. There are some 20 cultural, sports and recreational societies which are run voluntarily by the men and women of the village. These include a music society, theatrical society, mixed choir, folklore society, yodelling club, dancing group, clubs for shooting, ski-ing, tennis, swimming, football, curling and gymnastics, and last but not least a wrestling club (Schwingclub).

Special mention should also be made of the Alpine Rescue Squad (Rettungsstation) which forms part of the Swiss Alpine Club. The Alpine Rescue Squad is made up of experienced mountaineers from the Lenk community, who have volunteered to risk life and limb in the mountains should misfortune befall a climber or skier.

Perhaps the most active women's group in Lenk is the Women's Society (Frauenverein), whose president is Frau Rösli Gafner. It has a membership of some 300. Basically the Frauenverein concentrates on welfare work which includes visiting the sick in home and hospital, support for the needy and aged including meals on wheels, an old folks entertainment once a fortnight and presents at Christmas. No elderly person in Lenk need be lonely or in want. The Frauenverein also organizes courses in painting, woodcarving and other arts and crafts and also a course which prepares more ambitious elderly people for entry for university. All this social work of the Frauenverein is financed by voluntary subscriptions, a grant from the Commune, but more especially by the Brockenstube, a sale of clothes organised by the ladies of Lenk and held four times a year. Other clubs are the Landfrauenverein for farmers wives and interests itself in horticulture, and the swimming club for elderly ladies.

The majority of the adults in Lenk participate in community work in one way or another which no doubt accounts for the friendly atmosphere there. All this work is done on a voluntary or semi-voluntary basis.

Perhaps one of the best examples of public spiritedness in the Lenk community is that offered by Herr Emil Buchs, a former village school-master, who has given a lifetime's service to the village. One of three sons of a Lenk farmer, he decided early in life to enter the teaching profession. After studying at the village schools he went to a training college in Bern and on qualifying was appointed schoolmaster at the primary school in his own village. He filled that position for 42 years, in the course of which he became president of the Commune and a member of the Bern Cantonal Parliament. He served in that parliament, for which he received only a nominal reward, for 20 years until he retired a few years ago. After such a spell of public service he could have claimed, quite justifiably, that he had earned a quiet retirement, but he continued to serve his commune as billeting officer for Lenk.

Lenk has a barracks where Swiss militiamen do their refresher courses. In many other countries the military authorities would, no doubt, arrange for the billeting of troops, but in Switzerland this is done voluntarily by a local person. In Lenk Emil Buchs does the job. But it is not just a question of finding billets, he must also ensure that the necessary supplies of food are available. Nor do his duties finish here for he is required to keep an up-to-date register of the militiamen in the area, so that immediate mobilisation can be effected in an emergency, and he also acts as a welfare officer and deals with any personal problems which the men may have while doing their military service in Lenk.

When Emil Buchs was asked how patriotism and public spiritedness are taught to children in Switzerland, he said that it starts in the home and is supplemented in school. What he could have added, had he not been a modest man, was that perhaps they are learned even more effectively from the example set by public spirited people like himself.

The churches play an important part in encouraging Swiss youth to adopt a responsible attitude to the life of the commune by the teaching given in Sunday School and from the pulpit. The caring attitude displayed by the clergy and church communities towards their fellows also sets a fine example for the youngsters to follow, as does the work of the various religious interdenominational organizations such as Brot für Brüder and Fastenopfer in their humanitarian work overseas.

30

WENGEN

Wengen is another Swiss locality which can usefully serve as an example of Swiss political and social organization at a lower level. There are still traces here of Switzerland's Alemannic ancestry.

Like Lenk, Wengen is also a summer and winter sport resort in a most beautiful mountain setting. It is not a commune in itself but forms part of the Lauterbrunnen Commune. For centuries Wengen remained remote from the outside world and its development only really began when the Wengernalp railway was built at the end of the last century, and extended to the top of the Jungfrau in 1912.

The Alemannic tradition still remains in the form of joint ownership by the villagers of much of the land on the Männlichen mountainside on the east of the village which is a relic of the old Alemannic Allmend. Today this co-operative is called the Bäuertgemeinde and it has a closed membership of around 500 old Wengen inhabitants and membership is inherited.

The grazing land on the mountainsides was originally not only communally owned but also used communally by the people of Wengen. When, however, the use of common land was privatised in the middle of the 19th century, the ownership of the land was retained by the villagers but the grazing rights were leased to individual farmers for their exclusive use. This caused temporary hardship to the poorer villagers because they had nowhere to graze their cattle but it did mean that production could be stepped up and food shortages would be less likely.

The Bäuertgemeinde is a good example of joint endeavour. It is run democratically in that it has a general assembly which elects officials to run its affairs. All the offices are voluntary or semi-voluntary appointments and the profits which accrue are used to improve the amenities and environment of Wengen.

The Wengen Verkehrsverein is a second form of co-operative in the village. It is composed mostly of the hoteliers and business people of Wengen and has as its objective the improvement of the amenities of the village in order to make it more attractive as a holiday resort. It is financed from a visitors tax and by subscriptions from its various members. Once again it is democratically organized with a general assembly which appoints various committees to run its affairs. It is non-profit making and the various officials give of their time freely.

A third organization is the Frauenverein. It is organized in much the same way as in Lenk and does much the same work. The Frauenverein Movement was founded in 1888 to combat social distress and help both individuals and families in need. It now has some 300 branches throughout the country, is active in 18 cantons and has a membership of more than 80,000. It bodes well for the future that during the past six years 40 new branches have been founded and the majority of the members are young people.

In addition to its social work in the community the Frauenverein teaches handicrafts to female prisoners so that they may supplement the money they receive while serving their sentences. It also offers an advisory service to those with adopted children.

31

PARTNERSHIP WITH THE OUTSIDE WORLD

Partnership for Switzerland is not just a domestic matter - she also has close relations with foreign countries. One of the principles of Swiss foreign policy is universality, or that Switzerland should have diplomatic contacts with as many countries as possible, irrespective of the colour or complexion of their government.

A second principle of Swiss foreign policy is availability, namely that Switzerland should make her good offices available to any country in dispute. The fact that Switzerland is permanently neutral means that she can offer her services as mediator to foreign countries which are in dispute or at war and so keep dialogue and negotiations going between them. In 1982 she had mandates to represent 16 such nations.

Perhaps more important, however, is the assistance that Switzerland gives to the developing countries. Although not a member of the United Nations Organization, she co-operates closely in its humanitarian work and especially in that which involves the Third World.

Switzerland subscribes to Overseas Aid, both directly and indirectly through UNO agencies. Direct aid is offered in the form of financial assistance, technical aid and advice, and in trade measures such as preferential customs treatment for certain goods from the Third World. Switzerland has also developed her own programme for overseas humanitarian assistance in the event of natural catastrophe. Solidarity with the persecuted is shown by Switzerland's long record of offering asylum, when possible, and by her work for refugees.

Switzerland's permanent neutrality precludes participation in any treaty, offensive or defensive, which carries with it a risk of war.

Although Switzerland is not a member of the European Economic Community, she has a treaty of association with it. She is a member of the Council of Europe and of the European Free Trade Association, because this is purely a commercial association. Switzerland is also a member of the Organization for Economic Co-operation and Development, and she co-operates closely with the other leading industrial nations in matters of finance.

Many international organizations are domiciled in Switzerland, and perhaps the best known is the Red Cross. The Red Cross Movement was founded by a Swiss, Henri Dunant in 1864, to alleviate suffering in war. The International Red Cross Committee has its headquarters in Geneva and is made up solely of Swiss citizens. It is involved in humanitarian work and the upholding of human rights. There are some 130 national Red Cross associations affiliated to it. Switzerland is also a member of many other international organizations and, not least, acts as host to the World Council of Churches.

32

AGENCIES CONDUCIVE TO

PARTNERSHIP

FEDERALISM

Running right through Swiss social and political life are three forms of organization which have been conducive to the promotion of a spirit of partnership and co-operation among the Swiss people. The first and perhaps most important of these is federalism.

The Swiss Confederation, as stated earlier, is a federal country composed of 26 largely independant states called cantons and these are sub-divided into around 3,060 local authorities called communes. Political authority and administration is shared federally by these political entities.

Federalism has its disadvantages for it can make administration complicated, cumbersome and long drawn out. It can lead to discrepancies in legal and administrative interpretations, and thereby to inequalities. It has, however, many advantages, and above all it appears to be especially fitted to the Swiss conception of how their country should be administered. Federalism helps to provide an answer to the diversity and internal differences within Switzerland, which is composed of people speaking four different languages, with affinities to three different national cultures belonging to three different countries which border it. The Swiss people confess largely to two different religions. It is difficult to imagine how the country could survive for long if expression were not given to these differing elements through the channels that federalism makes available.

Federalism has also helped the development of democracy in Switzerland, because it has made possible experiments with democratic political innovations, such as the proportional representation voting system, at cantonal level before introducing them nationally. By extending democracy the individual's opportunities for involvement in political affairs have also been widened.

SUBSIDIARITY (SUBSIDIARITÄT)

A second organisational form operative in Switzerland is known in German as 'Subsidiarität' and to translate this word into English the word subsidiarity must be coined.

Subsidiarität is the word employed in West Germany, Austria and Switzerland to describe the precept, 'that no task shall be performed by a higher authority which could be executed equally well, or better, by a lesser or subsidiary authority' and as a corollary to this, 'that no higher authority should intervene with aid to a lesser authority until such time as the lesser authority can proceed no further by using only its own resources'.

Put in concrete form this means that in Switzerland no commitment shall be assigned to the Federal State which could be performed equally well or better by the cantons, nothing assigned to the cantons which could be performed equally well or better by the communes, and also that no function should be undertaken by any of these authorities which could be carried out equally well or better by the individual.

The aim of this principle of 'subsidiarity' is to allow the individual and the lesser political authorities to be free to run their own affairs without interference from above, until such time as their own resources are insufficient to execute the task. This view forms a basic element in the Swiss conception of freedom.

The implication of the application of this principle in the execution of political and social tasks is that a maximum amount of participation is reserved to the lesser authorities, and the fact that participation by the individual is closer and more widespread in these lower authorities means that the individual becomes more involved in the running of the country. Thus subsidiarity gives the citizen greater opportunity to serve his or her fellows.

The second great benefit that the application of subsidiarity confers is that it acts as safeguard against totalitarianism in a country. To lay stress on, and attach importance to what is subsidiary is the antithesis of the concept of centralised authoritarian rule by a higher authority.

Thus for a Swiss person the grades of importance of the various political authorities would appear to be reversed when compared with those in many other countries. An English equivalent to the Swiss conception would be if a Leeds person were to regard being a native of Leeds more important than being a Yorkshireman, and the latter of more importance than being English. Perhaps some do?

This strong sense of attachment to the local community is strengthened by the fact that each commune has its own flag and each valley its own local costume and customs. In the German speaking part of Switzerland each region, very often has its own dialect. Each community usually has its own choir and folk-dancing and music society. Folklore is given high priority in the local communities and many have their own folklore museums.

This attachment of the Swiss citizen to his commune is strengthened even more by the fact that the Federal Constitution stipulates the right of domicile to each Swiss citizen in his or her local commune, and also prescribes that the commune shall, where necessary, provide financial support and shelter in old age to each commune member. It is, therefore, to the commune that the Swiss citizen looks in times of necessity, rather than to the canton or to the the Federal State. This strong personal attachment to the local community is of value in that it promotes a closer involvement in local affairs.

This outlook will no doubt be criticised by many people as savouring of parochialism, and therefore of being detrimental to national unity, and so it can become if a balance is not kept between the relative requirements of the commune, canton and Federal State.

Yet this emphasis on the importance of the commune on the part of many Swiss people is usually accompanied by a deep sense of patriotism. This was brought home to me last summer when I visited the Rütli meadow on the shores of Lake Lucerne, where the Federal Oath was taken in 1291 which gave birth to the old Swiss Confederation. It was a warm day and the walk up to the memorial meadow earned refreshment in the form of a glass of beer. At the next table was an elderly Swiss man who obviously wished to talk.

'I came here first as an Army officer in 1940, when the Germans had tank divisions stationed at Pontarlier in France ready to invade Switzerland if given the command' he said, 'All Swiss officers over a certain rank were compelled to come here by our supreme commanding officer, General Guisan, and swear in the Rütli Meadow that we would fight to the death if Switzerland were invaded'.

'I have come back every year since the end of the War to renew my dedication to my country. This is my annual pilgrimage'.

In the meadow above us some 50 school children from Lausanne were being taught in French how their country was founded. Patriotism is inculcated early in life into Swiss people.

THE MILITIA SYSTEM

The third form of organization which permeates Swiss social and political life is what is known as the militia system. In the chapter describing the Swiss military organization the militia system of part time voluntary or semi-voluntary service figured prominently and as stated there, this unique form of organization is not confined to the Swiss Army but is evident in civilian life.

It is perhaps most manifest in the political field, because although the members of the Federal Government and certain members of the cantonal and commune governments are full time executives, there are no full time members of parliament in Switzerland. At all levels the Swiss parliaments are run militia-wise; that is part time in a voluntary or semi-voluntary capacity. This is even true of the two chambers of the Federal Parliament, namely the National Council and the States Council.

The Militia-system is also in evidence in the administration of Swiss law, in that the office of commune magistrate is a part time occupation and also the district courts and many of the cantonal courts are run militia-wise.

It should also be mentioned that many trade and professional organizations are run, at least partially, militia-wise and very many Swiss people serve on administrative or consultative committees, at all levels, in an honorary or semi-honorary capacity. This is also true of the administration of the numerous communally-owned co-operatives. It is also true to say that in Switzerland the militia-system is so widespread that it is regarded by many Swiss as the normal method of administrative organization.

33

ATTITUDES CONDUCIVE TO PARTNERSHIP

The incorporation of federalism, subsidiarity and the militia-system into the the organization and administration of Swiss political and social life ensures a close involvement of the Swiss people in the running of their country. This involvement can only be effective if right attitudes are adopted by these participants. The success, therefore, which Switzerland has had in developing from a land of penury to one with one of the highest standards of living in the world, full employment, a low inflation rate, a modest indigenous crime rate, and both external and industrial peace, must be attributable, in no small measure, to the adoption and development of correct attitudes by the Swiss people. A few of the more important attitudes will be cited here.

Perhaps one of the first things that strikes a foreigner on coming to live in Switzerland is the absence of aggressive behaviour on the part of the Swiss people. Acts of hooliganism and violence do occur but it is often the foreigners who seem to be responsible. The Swiss, for the most part, live peaceably together. This may be partly because they are not offensive to each other in a negative sense, by offering displays of ostentation which might humiliate their fellows. If a Swiss becomes rich, he or she does not appear to wish to flaunt their wealth, or use it to adopt a superior life style which would cut them off from their former friends, but seems inclined rather to tuck his

or her money away quietly in the bank and continue to
live much as before. In a sense, a Swiss man is compelled
to do this because the militia system insists that he still
does his military service with the same people and his
children are likely to continue at school with the same
classmates.

As a result of this continued participation in social life
by the successful members of the Swiss community, and as
a result of their mature attitude to wordly possessions, the
seeds of resentment and envy are less likely to be sown in
the minds of the less fortunate and consequently friction
does not seem to occur.

The policy of external non-aggression, which the Swiss
have pursued since they adopted a policy of neutrality in
the early 16th century may also have had an influence on
the adoption of non-aggressive political and industrial
policies inside the country.

It is perhaps more likely to stem, however, from a
second characteristic of the Swiss people, and that is a
willingness to compromise and to come to terms with
others. For the average Swiss, to reach agreement with an
adversary is the highest good. This spirit of compromise
is, perhaps best exemplified at political level by the
composition of the Federal Council which as we have seen
is a permanent coalition, consisting of two members from
the three largest political parties and one member from a
fourth party and is run on the principle of shared
responsibility. At industrial level it is best exemplified by
the signing of the Peace Agreement in the metal and
watch-making industry in 1937 and thereby the
acceptance of arbitration rather than confrontation. In
Switzerland not one whole day was lost in strikes in 1987.

This tradition of negotiation and mediation goes back
to the foundation of the old Swiss Confederation in the
Rütli meadow in 1291. The Federal Letter which was
signed there provides for the settling of disputes between
the Confederates. It clearly states that 'if discord should
arise between Swiss Confederates, then the most prudent
of the Swiss Confederates are to mediate and arbitrate in
the dispute, and if one of the parties should reject the
verdict of these arbitrators then the rest of the

Confederates must ensure that the verdict is complied with by the rebellious party'.

Closely connected with this willingness to compromise is the readiness on the part of many Swiss to co-operate with their fellows in joint endeavour for the good of the community and the nation in a voluntary or semi-voluntary capacity.

But perhaps the greatest contribution that a Swiss makes to the effective running of the country is his or her willingness to accept personal responsibility in political and social affairs.

34

SWITZERLAND'S UNIQUENESS

In what then precisely does Switzerland's uniqueness lie? Firstly in the extent to which democracy has been developed in Switzerland.

There are many countries in the world which vary considerably in their application of democracy, but I know of no other country where democracy has been experimented with so widely or developed so extensively as in Switzerland.

The introduction of the Referendum into the Swiss political system has meant that from then on every major piece of Swiss legislation may be made subject to a veto of the enfranchised Swiss citizens or cantons. In addition, the introduction of the Initiative has given the opportunity to both people and cantons to initiate legislation of which the Federal or cantonal government must take note. Thus the enfranchised citizens are sovereign, at least in theory.

Secondly Switzerland is unique in the extent of the involvement of her people in social and political affairs. This widespread involvement is a direct consequence of the comprehensive development of democracy cited above. I can think of no other country where the participation of the ordinary citizen in the running of the social, political and economic life of the country is so extensive. It is not only the extent of this participation which is remarkable, but the quality, in that, as we have seen, most of these social and political commitments are performed voluntarily or semi-voluntarily by Swiss men and women.

CONCLUSION

The Swiss have been fortunate in that historical and geographical circumstances have almost compelled them to evolve a political and social framework which encourages the development of political and social virtues. It is a framework which largely provides for the basic and natural requirements of the Swiss citizen, one which offers him or her a wealth of opportunity for self development, but at the same time makes provision for his or her reasonable participation and partnership in the running of the country's social and political life.

And as it is this active participation in common endeavour on behalf of the common good which promotes fellowship and comradeship, the participant is likely to find therein social satisfaction and contentment.

The question remains: 'Is this Swiss political and social system and practice exportable to other countries?'

I think the honest answer to that question must be 'in its entirety no', because each country has a different tradition and background.

But in that basic human needs are the same the world over, and political and social problems universal, it could well be that individual aspects of Swiss experience could be of benefit severally and in varying degrees to other countries. What is certain, however, is that those mature attitudes of non-aggression, compromise and personally responsible participation in political and social affairs, which the Swiss have developed over the years, are valid everywhere.